Teaching Your Kids to Care

How to Discover and Develop the Spirit of Charity in Your Children

Deborah Spaide

A Citadel Press Book
Published by Carol Publishing Group

Copyright © 1995 Deborah Spaide

Illustrations for Part I, Appendix I and Appendix II by Michelle Spaide. Illustration for Part II by Danielle Allen.

A Citadel Press Book
Published by Carol Publishing Group
Citadel Press is a registered trademark of Carol Communications, Inc.
Editorial Offices: 600 Madison Avenue, New York, N.Y. 10022
Sales and Distribution Offices: 120 Enterprise Avenue, Secaucus, N.J. 07094
In Canada: Canadian Manda Group, One Atlantic Avenue, Suite 105, Toronto, Ontario M6K 3E7
Queries regarding rights and permissions should be addressed to Carol Publishing Group, 600 Madison Avenue, New York, N.Y. 10022

Carol Publishing Group books are available at special discounts for bulk purchases, sales promotion, fund-raising, or educational purposes. Special editions can be created to specifications. For details, contact: Special Sales Department, Carol Publishing Group, 120 Enterprise Avenue, Secaucus, N.J. 07094

Manufactured in the United States of America
10   9   8   7   6   5   4   3   2   1

Library of Congress Cataloging-in-Publication Data

Spaide, Deborah.
    Teaching your kids to care : how to discover and develop the spirit of charity in your children / by Deborah Spaide.
        p.   cm.
    ''A Citadel Press book.''
    ISBN 0-8065-1637-2
        1. Children as volunteers—United States. 2. Social actions—Study and teaching—United States. 3. Charity—Study and teaching—United States. 4. Parenting—United States. I. Title.
HQ784.V64S63 1995
649.1—dc20
                                                              94-45271
                                                                 CIP

Contents

Acknowledgments

I would like to say thank you to the kids who contributed time and talent to this book: Danielle Allen and my daughter, Michelle, for their stick art, all the kids who were photographed in the midst of expressing their charity, and Katherine Lowe for sharing her courage and frustration with us, and teaching us that we are all more alike than we are different.

I would also like to thank all the adults who have started Kids Care Clubs and who have helped me to develop many of the projects in this book: Ann Campbell, Fran Dolan, Melanie Berman, Sara Marshall, Trudy Leddy, Debbie Owen, Erin Noonan, Janet Zaccarelli, Pat Groeschner, Paula Hannon, Susan Sievert, Maureen Hofer, and especially Cindy Princi for writing the two Kids Care skits in Project 100. And I would also like to thank Gary Fields, Attila Levi, David Abbey, and all the others who have supported and encouraged kids to help others through their schools and their example.

I would like to say thank you and I'm sorry to Paul and Nancy Heigl for reopening old wounds and sharing the pain and pride of their life with Jason.

I must also thank my father, my mother, and my grandmother, Mamie, who were always, and continue to be, the greatest examples of charity in my life.

A special thank-you to my husband for helping me develop the Kids Care Clubs and for his contributions of time, effort, and example to this cause. And I would like to thank my own five children: Michelle, Jennifer, Heather, Rebecca, and Christopher, for teaching me more about loving others than I could ever hope to teach them.

I would like to thank Mrs. Ramona Foran for her corrections and suggestions, and Dr. Cynthia Portal for her medical expertise.

Finally, I would like to thank the whispered voice of charity, which boldly promises all who will listen that the answer to our emptiness is not found in reaching up toward great success, but in reaching out to others who need us.

Introduction

This book began four years ago when my husband and I decided to introduce our five children to the benefits of helping others. We were invited to help repair a public housing apartment where an elderly woman lived. We spent hours washing, scraping, and painting walls. Everyone was tired, hungry and a little irritable. But when the woman returned to see our work later that day, we were all touched by her response. As we drove away, we began to brainstorm our next family project. We had shared something that day: the warmth of giving yourself away, the satisfaction of meeting a need, the camaraderie of working together as a team. Whatever it was, we wanted more.

The experience seemed especially important to our children. The next day, they went to school and told their friends what they had done. Some of their friends asked if they could help next time. We began making calls to find a need that this group of anxious do-gooders could meet. But no one wanted help from our kids! One organization suggested they stuff envelopes, and another offered to let the kids raise money for them. It didn't take long for us to realize that our society does not make it easy for children to develop their natural instinct for charity. Finally, we arranged to rake an elderly resident's lawn and fifteen kids showed up to help. Our theory reinforced, we began to search for meaningful ways that kids could interact with needy people in their community. That search became this book.

PART I

Developing the Spirit of
Charity in Children

CHAPTER 1

The Beginnings and Benefits of Charity

Most people think of charity as giving away money. But the original meaning of the word encompassed a great deal more than that. *Charity* is an ancient word that means to help others for the sake of love. Charity is hands-on love.

The spirit of charity exists in all of us from birth. It is the innate response to suffering reflected in the tears of a child when he hears a sad tale, or the unsolicited kindness of a child who shares his teddy with a frightened visitor. But as children grow older, they begin to get the message that they should not respond to suffering so openly. Society tells them that helping others is unsafe, unnecessary, or unwise. They are taught to restrain their charitable instincts and be realistic. It is the frustration of not being able to respond, of having to watch and accept human pain and suffering, that eventually hardens the hearts of our children.

Charity's first opportunities for expression are at home. Preschool children are notorious for trying to help, often with messy results. But despite appearances, they are not motivated by a need to make Mom's life more challenging; they are motivated by an instinct for charity. Little things, like getting a tissue for Dad, setting the table for

> *Charity is an ancient word that means to help others for the sake of love.*

5-year-old Chris Spaide sets the table for dinner.

dinner, or calling a grandparent on the phone, can make the child feel needed and involved. The initial opportunities for "reaching

6-year-old Lindsay Campbell helps her little brother.

out" within his or her family will provide a foundation for expanded charity as the child grows older.

Until the past few generations, life offered kids ample opportunity to exercise their charitable instincts. Extended families lived closer to one another, often with one another. Children were expected to help elderly grandparents, aunts, and uncles. The simplest home life required the help of all family members, even very young ones, to keep laundry washed, livestock fed, and fires burning. Some kids provided a primary source of income for the family's survival.

Thankfully, most American kids are not required to make such sacrifices for their families today. Child labor laws protect kids who work. Education laws mandate minimal schooling. That's good. But for all our progress on behalf of children, we lost something along the way. Our children lost the affirmation of being needed.

Why We Need to Help Others

A book called *The Healing Power of Doing Good* by Alan Luks and Peggy Payne[1] presents research on the health effects of volunteer service. They offer a remarkable argument for serving others as a means of improving our health. In researching several thousand volunteer organizations, they found the healthy effects were experienced in two distinct phases. The first was an immediate good feeling the authors called the "helper's high," which was present in 95 percent of the volunteers they researched. The second phase was associated with a sense of well-being, increased self-worth, serenity, and relaxation. This was likely to last for quite some time and be reexperienced when remembering the helping act. The authors assert that the calming effect of the second stage may contribute to the reduction of stress and stress-related illness.

The research done by Luks and Payne illustrates that humans are designed to respond to the needs of others. Charity is not completely selfless. Some sociologists call this helping instinct *reciprocal altruism,* and believe that humans (and some animals) help others with the expectation of some kind of return. Eastern religions speak of *karma* (or, to quote the Karate Kid, "What goes around comes around"). The book of Galatians in the Christian scriptures says, "You will reap whatever you sow (6:7)."

Lloyd C. Douglas referred to the helping instinct as a "magnificent obsession"[2] in his 1929 novel by the same name. In this wonderful story, Mr. Douglas reveals, with all the drama of a classic mystery, the secret of personal expansion. The following excerpt is an exchange between Randolph, who knows the secret, and Dr. Hudson, who wants to know it:

Randolph: Doctor Hudson, if you had a small, inadequate brick house, and decided to give yourself more room, what would you need for your building? . . . More brick. . . . If you had a small, inadequate steam-engine, you would want more steel to construct larger cylinders. . . .

Now, if you had a small, inadequate personality, and wanted to give it a chance to be something more important, where would you find the building materials?

Dr. Hudson: Well, according to the drift of your argument, I presume I would have to build it out of other personalities. Is that what you're driving at?

Randolph: Pre-cisely! But not "out of," INTO!

The secret Randolph was sharing with Dr. Hudson was that in order to enhance one's own self-worth, one must invest in others.

Magnificent Obsession also claimed that givers must never tell anyone about their gift or its value would be lost. While we don't suggest that kids do all their good deeds in secret, there is a certain purity of motive in giving secretly.

This past Christmas season our doorbell rang and our five kids ran from different corners of the house to be the first to answer it. But when they opened the door, no one was there. On the doormat they saw two ceramic candleholders with candles aglow inside and a stocking which contained a note. The note read: "The twelve days of Christmas are really neat! And just because we think you're sweet, we'll come and visit every night.

Children are quick to learn the secret of investing themselves in others.

But don't spy on us or we'll take flight. Your Christmas friend says 'Hi' to you, with gifts and treats we say . . . We Love You.''

Each night for the next eleven days, the doorbell would ring and a gift would be waiting on our doorstep. Sometimes it was a baked gift, sometimes it was a gift for one of the children, always it was inspiring. It made our Christmas more wonderful than ever, just knowing that someone cared enough to give us gifts, night after cold night, without the expectation of any return, or even a thank-you!

Most of the time it is not practical for kids to engage in secret giving, but the concept of giving without expectation of return should be encouraged in kids. There are many rewards for helping others beyond receiving a simple thank-you—the warmth of meeting a human need, the affirmation of contributing to society, and the reciprocal dignity of human compassion.

CHAPTER 2

Harvesting Human Dignity

E lizabeth Isler is the director of the Good Shepherd House of Hospitality in Norwalk, Connecticut. "Men have many hungers," reflects Elizabeth as she prepares a hot meal for 150 guests. Elizabeth likes to see flowers on the tables, fresh bread in the baskets, and smiles on the faces of volunteers. "Beauty is also a hunger," says Elizabeth. "Our guests love to see beauty." Elizabeth refuses to call Good Shepherd House of Hospitality

> *"Men have many hungers."*
> ELIZABETH ISLER

a soup kitchen. "We're glad you came" is their motto, and those who come are called guests. Guests are seated at tables and served restaurant-style by volunteers who bring them fresh salad, beverages, a main course, dessert, and a bag lunch to take with them. Elizabeth hopes they leave with more than just a meal each day. "We want them to know that we care for and honor them as people, whatever their status, whoever they are."

Respecting the dignity of the poor is essential because it is a contributing factor in breaking the cycle of poverty. Some social experts claim that poverty is the result of three factors: (1) isolation from other social classes and the benefits they enjoy, (2) lower acceptable standards of responsibility, and (3) expectations of failure.[3] When we choose to help the poor, we must consider how our help will register with them. Some poor are embarrassed to accept our help. Some are angry at their bad luck (and therefore angry with anyone who has good luck). Some are so engrossed in their effort to survive that common courtesy has no place on their priority list. The last thing these human beings need is to be asked to jump through more hoops by do-gooders.

When charity is at its best, it not only meets the need of the moment, but also plants seeds of hope for the future. Reaching out to those in need helps the children of advantage interact with the children of disadvantage. It helps break down the barriers of class. It helps the needy

> *When charity is at its best, it not only meets the need of the moment, but also plants seeds of hope for the future.*

begin to recognize their worth, and it helps the children begin to realize their ability to make a contribution.

Most kids can relate to the degradation of being unrecognized as important human contributors. If you want some hard lessons in humiliation, just follow a teenager around for a day. I can't count the times I've watched a store clerk ignore a teenager waiting for assistance in deference to adults who just walked in. Perhaps this attitude is a result of capitalism (focus on the biggest buck), but more likely it is simply youthism. Our developed society tends to place a lower value on the contribution of its children than most developing countries do.

Six-year-old Casey went with a group of children to tour a homeless shelter. Casey learned that some families lose their homes and have to live in a shelter while they find a new home. After the tour the guide asked the children if they had any questions. Casey raised her hand and

> *"Where do the pets of homeless children go to live?"*
>
> CASEY DOLAN

asked, "Where do the pets of homeless children go to live?" The guide laughed and said, "I don't know. God, I can hardly take care of the kids!"

Casey went home thinking she had asked a stupid question. She had been humiliated in front of her friends and was determined to keep her mouth shut next time. The guide didn't intend to make Casey feel that way, but she failed to consider Casey's question from the perspective of a young child. Many kids adore their pets, and leaving them would be more traumatic than leaving their homes. What does happen to homeless pets? I imagine that children who, in the process of homelessness, are separated from their pets, might suffer from feelings similar to the death of a loved one. How could society be so insensitive to its children? It takes the insight of a child like Casey to illuminate the indifference of adults. How desperately we need the contribution of our children!

As we teach our children how to respond to the call of charity, we are showing them that we value their contributions. As we tell others about their concerns and their efforts, we are affirming their individual and corporate dignity, rejecting youthism, and perhaps making a difference in the way our society treats its young people in the future.

CHAPTER 3

Empowering Kids to Reach Out

There is nothing new about inviting kids to help with social issues. Adults have been involving kids in fund-raising drives for decades. What is new is empowering kids to be the leaders in social change. Kids are amazing. They can understand difficult social problems, and they are very creative with solutions. They have many answers that have eluded us older folk. They are exploding with creativity, with untapped energy, with innocent determination, and with genuine kindness. Empowered children will grow to be empowered adults, parents, and citizens. This new generation will transcend the "me-ism" of the seventies and eighties. They will see the world differently, and interpret social situations with concern for mankind—not status. Perhaps through our children we can start an epidemic of human kindness.

Empowered Kids Are Not Sheltered From Problems

A necessary component of charity is the ability to feel someone else's pain. It is painful to see a hungry young child with bony legs and pleading eyes. The spirit of charity makes us imagine

> *A necessary component of charity is pain.*

what someone else might feel, how he might hurt, how desperately he must hope for help. All this happens in a moment, and in that moment we are given a choice: Do we respond to charity's call or ignore it?

The choice that charity presents is laden with frustrations. "Even if I choose to help, would my contribution matter in the face of such a large problem?" "How can I help?" "If I choose to give money, whom can I trust to use my money honestly?" Many conscientious adults opt to ignore the suffering because they are frustrated by the opportunities to help.

This frustration is more pervasive among children. In our age of instant technology, kids are exposed to more suffering than any

> *In our age of instant technology, kids are exposed to more suffering than any generation before them.*

generation before them. They can daily tune in to real-life death, mutilation, starvation, crime, war, and injustice. And that's just the evening news. Yet children have fewer resources with which to respond to what they see than adults do. Most have no income, so they can't write a check. Most depend on the transportation provided by adults to go anywhere. When kids see starving children on TV, they are forced to feel the pain of that child without any hope of helping him.

Kids can only go on for so long, feeling such painful empathy without any opportunity to do anything about it, before they begin to tell themselves to stop feeling anything at all.

Many parents try to protect their kids from the pain of charity. When American troops went to Somalia to bring food to the starving people there, a radio show interviewed several wives of the soldiers involved in the operation. The announcer asked one wife how her children were reacting to seeing the soldiers at work in Somalia on the news. The mother responded that they were not allowed to watch the news because she didn't want them to see the starving children. That mom knew her children would experience pain if they witnessed the horror of starvation, so her solution was to prevent them from witnessing it.

Preventing children from witnessing the suffering of others is one way to distance them from the pain of charity. And there are times when distance is a wise option for parents of young children, as in the case of rape or massacre. But distance from charity is not an empowering response to problems; it is a dishonest denial that problems exist. In the case of the dad in Somalia, an honest and empowering response would have been for the mom to allow her children to see the problem, feel the pain, and find opportunities to help. Perhaps the kids could have started a food drive in school and sent the food to Somalia with the next crew. Or perhaps the kids could have sent "keep up the good work" cards to the soldiers who were in Somalia. The end result of their efforts may not have solved the starvation in Somalia, but the children would have learned that they could make a difference.

While TV exposes kids to a wide variety of social problems, sometimes they need more tangible experiences. The benefits of visiting soup kitchens, homeless shelters, hospitals, AIDS facilities, low-income day-care centers, or nursing homes are enormous for kids. They learn that the victims of homelessness and illness are just like them in many ways. Several teenage girls who spent a Saturday afternoon serving lunch at a homeless shelter and playing with the homeless children remarked later that the homeless people they met were better off than they were because "they know how to be happy without lots of things." "I guess I'll think twice before I tell my mom that I'll just die unless I get that new skirt," said one of the girls. These kids were exposed to the real people behind the real problems, and they were touched, perhaps changed, by their experience.

> *"I guess I'll think twice before I tell my mom that I'll just die unless I get that new skirt."*
>
> KATIE CHECKETTS

Empowered Kids Conceive the Solutions Themselves

Most kids envision a barrage of solutions after being exposed to a problem. That's the nature of kids. They innocently believe that everything can be fixed. They put themselves in the shoes of the sufferer and consider what they would feel like in that circumstance, and what would make them feel better. A group of first graders heard a story about homelessness and were asked what they could do to help homeless kids. One enthusiastic little girl said, "We could buy them Roller Babies." (Roller Babies are battery-operated dolls that skate; they sell for forty dollars or so.) While the little girl's suggestion may not have been practical, it was a response to sincere empathy. She imagined herself without a home and she felt sad, she then considered what would make her happy, and she thought of a Roller Baby. That is the beginning of empathy. The adult involved in the discussion handled the situation expertly by turning to the little girl and acknowledging that Roller Babies would make homeless children happy. Then she asked the class, "What do the rest of you think of giving the homeless children Roller Babies?" Some thought it was a great idea, but other kids remarked that homeless boys might not like them. Meanwhile, one of the kids suggested a food gift. The adult led the discussion in the direction of the food gift and made a special effort to include the little girl with the Roller Baby idea.

Kids need to have ownership in the solution. It is empowering to see a problem, think of a solution, and realize the success of your own idea. Following a prescribed agenda dictated by adults doesn't feel the same to kids. It sends a message of dependence to kids, instead of a message of competence.

Kids' ideas are not as practical as adults', but that is part of their magic. Their minds are not yet clouded with the logic that imprisons adults. They are free to consider all the possibilities, to explore all the angles. They need adults to gently steer them by affirming their ideas and asking practical questions.

Empowered Kids Learn From Their Experiences

The field of charity is large enough to offer kids a variety of opportunities and a smorgasbord of lessons about life. Charity helps kids discover their talents, hone their skills, and begin to believe in themselves. Academic lessons in math, science, reading, writing, and social studies can be integrated into meaningful service projects. Helping others can teach kids about citizenship, cooperation, processing experiences, respect for life, problem solving, and about their own strengths and weaknesses. A group of kids made lunch for a family homeless shelter one Saturday afternoon. While lunch was being prepared by some of the kids, others were sent into the game room to entertain the little children living there. All of the students enjoyed the opportunity to play with the children, but one

> *Charity helps kids discover their talents, hone their skills, and begin to believe in themselves.*

quiet student discovered her special ability to interact with preschool children. Other kids may learn how to paint or build houses, bake, organize projects, be leaders, advertise events, speak in public, and work cooperatively with others.

Charity can teach kids about good stewardship of what they have. We all have something to share with others who have less. Our good health can be shared with others in poor health. Our energy can be shared with others who are tired from life's trials. Our hope can be shared with others who have lost hope. Our time can be shared with others who feel unloved. Our eyes can be shared with others who have lost their sight. The list is endless. We all have something that we can share.

Charity can teach kids antimaterialism. Charity is *process*-oriented, not *product*-oriented. Mother Teresa was once asked why she kept caring for the sick when she knew that no matter what she did, they would still die. Mother Teresa said, ''Whether they live or die is irrelevant to the act of love.'' Mother Teresa was responding to the principle of charity. The final product was not her focus; the act of love was itself a worthy outcome.

Charity can teach kids moral values. It helps kids move their focus from themselves to the larger community. It helps them develop ideals and teaches them to apply what they believe in. Charity builds character in kids because it strengthens the center of their self-identity. Kids learn that it feels good to do the right thing, and that makes it easier for them to say no to the wrong thing. Kids find their personal worth is affirmed in their kindness toward others, so they don't need to search for worth in drugs, sex, or crime.

> *Kids find their personal worth is affirmed in their kindness toward others, so they don't need to search for worth in drugs, sex, or crime.*

Empowered Kids React to Human Need

There are many different ways for kids to volunteer. They can join an organization like the Red Cross, they can become environmentally active, they can work for community improvements, or they can simply reach out to someone who needs them. It is usually more beneficial for kids to focus on meeting human needs than fund-raising or community improvement efforts. For example, a group in Connecticut decided to improve the public park in their community. In no time, the group had successfully raised several thousand dollars for a new playground. This was a fun and rewarding experience for all who became involved. However, the project was a community improvement effort for an affluent population; it was not a direct response to a human need.

A litter pick-up day was planned in a small town by a group of kids. The kids were veteran volunteers, having planned and executed many other service projects successfully. Many kids had always turned out to help with projects in the past, often canceling other plans because helping others was more important. But when

Katie Heigl enjoys helping others who need her.

the day scheduled for the litter project arrived, only six kids came. Picking up trash around their little town didn't have the same meaning for them as preparing a meal for homeless kids. They agreed it was important to keep their town beautiful, but they weren't willing to give up their Saturday to do it. It didn't satisfy a human need.

Empowered Kids See the Results of Their Work

It is not enough to be told that you are doing a good thing; kids need to be able to see it for themselves. For example, stuffing envelopes for a fund-raiser would not be very fulfilling. Making bag lunches for homeless people is great, but it would be greater if the kids could meet the homeless people they were making sandwiches for. Buying new toys for the day-care center is wonderful, but would be more wonderful if the kids could watch the toys being enjoyed by the little children at the day-care center.

THE CIRCLES OF CHARITY

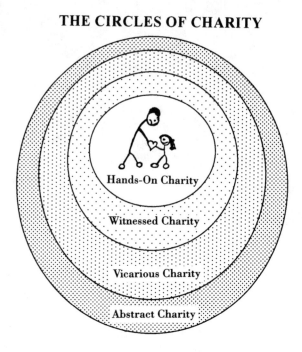

Hands-On Charity

Witnessed Charity

Vicarious Charity

Abstract Charity

The Circles of Charity (above) illustrates the different impact that charity projects can have on children. The most desirable charity experience for children is represented by the center circle, Hands-on Charity. Experiences that put children in direct contact with the recipients of their efforts, like working in a soup kitchen, are experiences that allow children to directly touch a human need. The second circle of charity is Witnessed Charity. This circle includes activities that allow kids to see the people they are helping, but not to have any interaction with them. An example of Witnessed Charity is making bag lunches for a soup kitchen, but not staying to pass them out to the people who will eat them. The third circle is Vicarious Charity. This type of charity is dependent on others to carry it out. Vicarious Charity takes place when kids collect toys for an organization to deliver to another country. The kids may see photos of the children receiving the toys, but the giving is done by others. The last circle of charity is Abstract Charity. Abstract Charity is also the largest circle because it is where the most opportunities are found. Giving money to organizations that will help the needy is a type of Abstract Charity. The giver is uncertain of how the money will be used and has no contact with the recipient of their gift.

(A type of charity not mentioned in this illustration is Structural Charity. Structural Charity works through activism, politics, and literature to incite social reforms that would benefit the needy. This type of charity requires an understanding of complex issues and the inner strength to withstand many disappointments. Some high school students are capable of meaningful Structural Charity and entire curriculums have been designed on this subject at the college level.)

The Circles of Charity should cause us to question the value of fund-raising activities for children. Raising money is not directly connected to meeting a human need. Seeing a lot of cash in a shoe box after a car wash may feel good, but it doesn't satisfy the spirit of charity. It requires too much abstraction for kids to imagine the money turning into biscuits for hungry children. But what if the kids took the money they earned at the car wash and went shopping for food, then delivered the food to a soup kitchen, and even helped to serve the food they bought? That would be a very empowering experience for the kids.

Sometimes it isn't possible for kids to see the results of their work firsthand, for example, helping starving children abroad. This places an added burden on the adult to find ways to make the kids realize the importance of their contribution. This can be done by getting quotes from the recipients and passing them on to the kids, or getting photos if possible.

Seven-year-old Elizabeth heard that prisoners' children often don't get Christmas gifts. Her mom got the name and phone number of a prisoner's child from Prison Fellowship. (Prison Fellowship is Charles Colson's ministry to prison inmates. See Appendix I.) Elizabeth sent a present to a child whose dad was in jail. On Christmas morning, Elizabeth received an excited phone call from the prisoner's daughter. Her most memorable gift that Christmas came from a brand new friend whom she had never met, who called to say "Thank you for caring about me."

CHAPTER 4

Caring Is Contagious

The Kids Care Club Story

Kids Care Club is a group of kids who want to have fun to-gether while they help others. The first Kids Care Club started in New Canaan, Connecticut, with eighteen kids.

The Kids Care Club actually started itself. One spring week-end in 1990, our family decided to help an elderly widow clean her lawn and plant some flowers. When our kids told their friends about the project, many of them wanted to help too. On Saturday morning fifteen kids showed up at our door with rakes and en-thusiasm. Many had canceled other plans because "this was more important." We called neighbors to help us drive and headed to the elderly widow's home.

On the drive, Jim confessed that he anticipated little work would get done. "The kids will be fooling around, and we'll have to watch them instead of doing the work," he predicted. When we arrived at Mrs. Luckhurst's house, she was overwhelmed by all the young helpers. She whispered, "God must be rewarding me for teaching Sunday school all those years!"

In a few hours the yard was raked clean, and pink flowers were planted around Mrs. Luckhurst's patio and mailbox. The kids worked hard. Jim was happy to admit that he'd been wrong. The kids made Mrs. Luckhurst feel remembered and cared for. They met a human need.

Mrs. Luckhurst with some members of the first Kids Care Club.

The next project of the Kids Care Club was making bag lunches for a local soup kitchen. The kids each brought a loaf of bread, and local markets donated fresh fruit, peanut butter, jelly, and cookies. Twenty-five kids turned out to help with this project. Some decorated the lunch bags with crayons and markers, while others formed assembly lines to make sandwiches and fill the lunch bags with fruit and cookies. In forty-five minutes the kids made 150 bag lunches, which were delivered to the soup kitchen that same day. Later, we heard that the children who ate at the soup kitchen that night were thrilled with the colorful bags. "After they ate the lunches, they saved the pretty bags!" reported one volunteer.

> *Kids Care Clubs are a testimony to the hunger our children have to help others.*

Since then, the kids have planned and successfully completed many charity projects. Their example led five public schools in New Canaan to adopt Kids Care Clubs as organized school activities. Word has spread beyond town lines, and today Kids Care Clubs are starting in neighborhoods and churches too. Kids Care Clubs are a testimony to the hunger our children have to help others. (To start a Kids Care Club, see Chapter 5, Project 1.)

Trevor Ferrel discovered how quickly the spirit of charity could spread when he was eleven years old. After watching a news broadcast about homeless people, Trevor wanted to give them blankets. He piled some old blankets by the door and then, for almost an hour he pleaded with his parents to drive him to Philadelphia. As a last resort, he made up a contract to do his homework every night for a week. That worked. Trevor's parents helped him load the car and drove him into the shaded streets of Philadelphia where homeless people lived. Trevor got out of the car and gave an old man who was lying on a sidewalk grate one of the blankets. The look in that old man's eyes changed Trevor's life. Every night thereafter he and his family loaded their car with blankets and sandwiches and headed for Philadelphia's streets. Others heard about the trips and donated food, supplies, and transportation to Trevor's cause. Ten years later the movement has outgrown the family car and operates from a building on Westchester Pike called Trevor's Place. Every day, volunteers serve 250 hot meals at Trevor's Place and make warm beds for eighty homeless people to sleep in. Nineteen chapters of Trevor's Campaign for the Homeless have started in other parts of the country, and two abroad.

As further evidence of the need our kids have to help others, a Gallup Poll was recently commissioned by the Independent Sector, a nonprofit coalition in Washington, D.C., to survey volunteerism among American teenagers. The survey found that 61 percent of American teenagers were volunteering on a weekly basis, compared to 51 percent of American adults. The contribution made by these teenagers was valued at more than seven billion dollars! The Independent Sector

> *"American teenagers, often criticized for lack of caring and commitment, are volunteering at the same rate as adults."*
>
> THE INDEPENDENT SECTOR

was so impressed with their findings that they issued a news release which stated, ''American teenagers, often criticized for lack of caring and commitment, are volunteering at the same rate as adults and also sharing their limited financial resources to help others.'' Here are some of the ways that kids are spending their time and money to spread the spirit of charity:

Third Graders at Polk-Hordville School

Mrs. Wurst has an unusual curriculum for her third-grade students at Polk-Hordville Public School in Polk, Nebraska. Every morning the entire class gathers and calls nineteen elderly men and women to say good morning and to make sure they have heat and food for the day. The kids also meet their elderly friends twice a year at a Christmas party and a spring tea. Many of the students develop relationships with their elderly friends and visit them after school and on weekends.

Little Vikings

High school students at Lamar High School in Arlington, Texas, wanted to help disadvantaged kids complete their education. They developed a program called Little Vikings to assist grade school kids who were identified as potential dropouts. Each Little Viking is matched with a high school kid. The high school student tutors and develops a friendship with his Little Viking. So far, the Little Vikings are responding with affection, academic success, and increased self-confidence.

The Kerby Sisters

Beth, Kerry, and Megan Kerby live in Troy, Michigan. These sisters are committed to helping mentally retarded children. Beth, aged thirteen, Kerry, aged eleven, and Megan, aged eight, work at the Wing Lake Development Center for retarded children. Their duties include playing with handicapped children and assisting them with activities. The Kerby sisters provide the kids at Wing Lake with an opportunity to interact with peers and to experience friendships.

Teens Against Child Abuse

Shelley Joyce Spell is a surviving victim of child abuse. She lives in Houston, Texas, where she founded a group called Teens Against Child Abuse (TACA). TACA is a support group for other kids who are being abused or who have been abused in the past. In addition to support for victims, the group also works with schools and law enforcement agents to promote public awareness of child abuse.

Reachout to Seniors

David Lessen first experienced the gratification of helping others as a high school student in Woodmere, New Jersey. His first project was to help a senior citizen. He decided to develop a program to help other teens discover the satisfaction of charity. David designed a program called Reachout to Seniors, which he introduced at his high school. David and other high school students regularly help the elderly residents with chores like changing lightbulbs, turning mattresses, storing things on high shelves, caulking windows, and fixing broken items.

Kids Against Crime

In 1985, when Linda Warsaw was twelve years old, she founded Kids Against Crime in San Bernardino, California. Linda volunteered to help with the Victim Witness Assistance Program of the San Bernardino County District Attorney's Office. Through her work with the victim witness program, Linda became aware of crimes involving abuse, kidnapping, and child molestation. Linda decided to help kids learn how to protect themselves. Kids Against

Crime teaches kids how to prevent a crime, and what to do if they are involved in or witness a crime. Linda's group operates a hot line and provides public awareness information.

WillSERVE

The Williamsport Students Engaged in Real Volunteer Efforts (WillSERVE) is comprised of 164 high school students in Williamsport, Pennsylvania. The students tutor local grade school kids, help senior citizens, help at the local hospital, and serve twelve community service organizations. Altogether, the kids contribute almost one thousand hours of volunteer service to their community per month.

Boy Scout Troop 4

The kids in Boy Scout Troop 4 of Ann Arbor, Michigan, are real clowns. The boys have been trained in clown ministry and use their skills to bring smiles to senior citizens at local nursing homes. They also spend time manicuring and beautifying the grounds of the nursing homes. One of the boys even designed a wheelchair-accessible miniature golf course! The scouts are now planning to build a wildlife sanctuary.

4-H Search and Rescue Cadets

The ten members of the Warm Springs, Oregon, Search and Rescue Cadet program risk their own lives to rescue others. The young members, aged ten to eighteen, work along with the Jefferson County Search and Rescue Team and are treated as professionals by their adult counterparts. They are trained in swift water rescue, CPR, first aid, and wilderness survival. This year the cadets have participated in twelve rescue operations. Their tasks include tracking missing persons, recovering bodies, investigating murder scenes, and assisting with the care of injured persons.

Directing Charity Projects
With a Group of Kids

From your family around the kitchen table, to a structured Kids Care Club with several hundred members, the development of charity requires adults to stand back and let the kids respond to the needs of their world. Let the kids choose the projects, organize, and do the work. Adults works backstage to encourage, support, and protect the kids.

Possibly the most important role of the adult is to protect the kids from things which frustrate the work of charity. Complaints, thoughtless comments, bureaucratic red tape, and the hidden agendas of larger organizations are debilitating to adults, but for children they can be fatal to the shy spark of charity.

While visiting a local homeless shelter, a Kids Care Club noticed that the children who lived there had very little to play with in the yard. After a talk with the shelter supervisor, the kids decided to have a car wash and earn money to buy a small plastic climbing gym.

The kids worked hard one entire Saturday without even a break for lunch, washing a long line of dirty cars and vans and even a boat. They had reason to be proud when they reached their goal. But when a call was made to the shelter to arrange for delivery and setup of the new climbing gym, a different voice answered the phone. The supervisor had said a climbing gym would be great, but this voice said ''A climbing gym was inappropriate for the shelter. No thanks!'' The Kids Care Club adult knew how disappointed the kids were going to be. After a tense conversation with the shelter employee, it was agreed that the climbing gym would be returned to the toy store and the kids would shop for some indoor games and books instead. The kids went shopping and delivered bags of toys to the shelter. The project was salvaged and the kids never knew how close it came to disaster.

This Kids Care Club car wash earned $150 to buy toys for homeless kids.

Applying a Principle

Charity projects help kids to internalize and energize a belief system. Adults should offer kids the opportunity to verbalize and define their developing principles of human kindness and social justice. For many kids the feelings gain power and significance when they are spoken out loud.

> *Charity projects help kids to internalize and energize a belief system.*

Americares, an international relief organization based in New Canaan, Connecticut, asked Kids Care Clubs to help them collect children's books for homeless shelters in New York City. The kids agreed, and their first project was designing book drop boxes to leave around town. While they stenciled letters on the boxes,

they talked about why they wanted to collect books for children.
Here are some of the things they had to say:

*It is important because a lot of kids don't have as much
as we have.*—Lindsey Boland

*People who have so much don't appreciate it. We waste
too much.*—Tori Sterkin

I just like helping other people.—Daniel Pattenden

*We like reading books, and we want other kids to like
them too.*— Jessica Tiani

I don't think anyone should live in poverty.—Bently Elliot

*We have so much. It is good to give things to people who
don't.*—Holly Retz

We are sending books to kids so they can learn.—Beth
Wieber

I hope new books will be exciting for them.—Kathryn
Archer

It isn't fair that we have so much and they have so little.—
Katie Lane

*Books provide a source of education and entertain-
ment.*—Alison Green

We should care about others who are less fortunate.—
Rachel John and Jessica Tiani

Kids deserve books!—Tamar Gertner

PART II

Human Kindness Projects for Kids

Dear Parents, Teachers, and Youth Leaders,

The following pages are written to help you develop the spirit of charity in children. There are more than one hundred projects listed, and in some cases a project will offer several different options for kids to choose from. They are divided into charity chapters: The Poor, The Children, The Elderly, The Handicapped, and Injustice. Each charity chapter begins with a short story and a brief lesson on that group of people, followed by project ideas to serve their needs.

At the top of each project listing is a box which tells you how much time the project might take, what skills or materials are needed to accomplish the project, and what grade level the project is best suited to. Because some of the projects will have associated expenses, there is also a chapter on fund-raising activities.

I would like to apologize ahead of time to the adults who read these project instructions and find the details a celebration of the obvious. It was a conflict, as I wrote the instructions, to address you or to address your children. I decided to write in a language and format that was most accessible to the children. It was my hope that the children would read about the projects themselves, instead of relying on an adult to interpret each one for them. I hope these projects will be a springboard for your children to conceive of their own projects and ideas.

While I tried to be comprehensive, I am sure I have forgotten important details and will rely on the adults who supervise these projects to determine what is missing. I ask you to consider any project your child participates in carefully, with an overcautious focus on safety. Please think through each project and determine what measures are necessary to make the project successful and safe for everyone.

I would love to hear your comments and your experiences with the development of charity in your children. I would also like to hear about any unusual twists that your children gave these projects, or about other projects they created. You can write to me at:

Deborah Spaide
c/o Carol Publishing
600 Madison Ave.
New York, NY 10022

CHAPTER 5

Understanding the Poor

Raphael's Revenge

It was raining hard when the cars pulled up in front of the gray concrete building. A small rusty sign over the door read 'The Good Shepherd House of Hospitality.' There was no obvious place to park, so the cars edged over the curb, carefully dodging the whiskey bottle wrapped in brown paper.

Six car doors opened simultaneously and seventeen teenagers catapulted onto the sidewalk. They were coming from the New Canaan Kids Care Club, innocently anxious to share their good will and cold macaroni and cheese with the less fortunate guests of the Good Shepherd House.

The doors to the building were locked, and the windows were shaded and barred. The adults in the group held bags over their heads to deflect the rain and pounded feverishly on the door. The kids, ignoring the rain, made friends with an old man who was sitting on the soggy ground beside the doorway.

The door flung open and a man who looked like a retired football player motioned the group inside. The old man stood up to follow them, but the football player stopped him. ''Not until three-thirty, Joe,'' he said. The confused old man dropped his head and returned to his place in the rain.

It was Christmas season, and the kids had brought bags of decorating materials. With their bags unpacked and their sleeves rolled up, the kids cut and taped red, green, and white streamers from all the doorways and hung big foil stars from the suspended ceiling. Red carnations, white daisies, and baby's breath were arranged in empty soda bottles to become pretty centerpieces for bare tables sprinkled with colored confetti. One of the kids, named Mike, knew how to play the piano. He sat down at an old piano that someone had donated to the soup kitchen, and began to play Christmas carols. The music, more than any of the decorations, dissolved the gray hue of the room into a golden softness.

While the kids worked inside, 150 homeless guests lined up outside. At precisely 3:30 P.M., the football player opened the doors, and the guests rushed in out of the rain, shaking like cats after a bath. They all knew the routine and each other. They had been coming to Good Shepherd House every day for a hot meal. The kids were the strangers in the room. The guests seated themselves in brown metal chairs at long folding tables and waited to be served their meal. The kids served macaroni and cheese, meatballs, salad, rolls, and fresh fruit. After their meal, each guest received a hunk of white cake which the kids had made and decorated the night before, and a bag lunch to take along for later.

It didn't take long for the kids to be accepted by the guests. The young children who came to eat there were especially happy to have other kids around. Seven-year-old Jermaine challenged one of the Kids Care kids to a game of Fish. Fifteen-year-old Rachel met his challenge and suffered an embarrassing defeat. Several of the youngest guests had so much fun that they asked if they could help clean up the kitchen after the meal.

But the surprise of the afternoon came from a handsome young guest named Raphael. When Mike took a break from the piano, Raphael sat down and ran his fingers across the keys.

"May I play?" he asked one of the kids. But when the kids invited him to sit down at the piano, he looked worried.

"I can't read," he said.

"Perhaps you could play by ear," suggested someone.

Raphael was amused by the term "play by ear" and tugged

*at his ears teasingly as he whistled a tune. The kids all laughed.
And with the echo of laughter still lingering, Raphael turned his
determined eyes to the keys. He stretched out his hands in front
of him, as if in homage to the old piano, and then slowly lowered
them. As his fingers touched the keys they became a sudden blur,
moving gracefully to and fro from melody to melody.*

*"Any requests?" he asked with a grin. Raphael was a very
talented pianist! Before long, Raphael had all the kids and all the
guests singing along to tunes like "Lean on Me" and "Heat
Wave."*

*The kids worked hard that day, and many complained of aching
feet on the drive home. But they had learned about homeless
people. They learned that homeless people are real people, some
with real talents, who for one reason or another have no place to
live. "It was fun," said one Kids Care member. "Let's do it
again," said others. All agreed that the pain in their feet was a
small price to pay for the warmth in their hearts.*

Who Are the Poor?

Many families are classified as poor although one or both parents
work. There are 2.8 million working poor, according to the U.S.
Census Bureau, and 32.5 million people living below the poverty
level. A full-time job at minimum wage yields an income that is
below the poverty line for a family of four.[4] These families may
have enough income to keep a small apartment or home, but cannot afford to keep food in their
cabinets, and they are often without phones, heat, or other necessities. Some of these families are
evicted from their homes and left
on the street to fend for them-
selves. Thirty-three percent of all homeless Americans are families with children; twenty-five percent are children.[5]

> *Thirty-three percent of all
> homeless Americans are
> families with children;
> twenty-five percent are
> children.*

The Food Research and Action Center in Washington, D.C., claims that as many as 5.5 million children are hungry in the United States each day. The poor can receive food stamps from the government; however, the food stamps may not last the entire month. They can also eat meals at local soup kitchens if they live close to one, but many poor families live in rural communities, miles from the nearest soup kitchen. And most soup kitchens serve only one meal a day, which will not meet the nutritional needs of children.

A large number of the poor are single mothers with children, many of whom began motherhood during their teenage years. Incomplete education and the lack of affordable day care make the cycle of poverty hard to break for families. Many of these moms were abused as children or battered by their mates. Most of these moms struggle to make a life for their children and fight the social misconceptions about their humiliating position.

Other poor people live on the streets or in homeless shelters. It is hard to get a definite count of homeless people, since they have no addresses to send the census forms to, but the estimates range between 300,000 and 3 million people who survive without homes or secure shelter. Homeless shelters provide only a small portion of the beds needed to accommodate homeless people.

Who are these people who live in shelters and eat at soup kitchens or even from trash cans? They are people just like you and me. They end up in the dehumanizing frustration of poverty through various experiences and choices. Some are drug or alcohol addicted, some are uneducated or illiterate, some are mentally or emotionally handicapped, some are raising children without a partner or support system, some are not U.S. citizens and are unable to apply for government aid, some are victims of low wages or the economy, and some simply don't believe they can do any better.

Here are some statistics[6] about homeless people to consider:

- 33 percent are families with children

- 25 percent are children

- 20 percent are mentally or emotionally ill
- 25 percent have drug- or alcohol-related problems
- 54 percent are nonwhite
- 48 percent have no high school education
- 30 percent hold jobs
- 35 percent are veterans
- 50 percent are severely depressed
- 20 percent have attempted suicide (women with children are five times more likely to attempt suicide)

Let me tell you about Audrey. She is thirty-three years old, a retail sales clerk, the mother of a fifteen-year-old boy, and she is homeless. Audrey lost her job four months ago, and she remains unemployed though she is determined to find a job and get off welfare. She sent her son to live with her mother in another state to keep him out of the homeless shelter that she has lived in for the past four months. She did what she thought was best for her son, but it has not been the best move for Audrey. Audrey is frustrated by the lack of services for single homeless people. Mothers with children are encouraged to apply for jobs and look for apartments. The shelter owns a van which is driven by volunteers to transport homeless mothers to job interviews. But the van is not available to Audrey because her son isn't living with her. She feels the system encourages prolonged homelessness and promotes laziness.

Audrey will make it. She is smart, determined, and has marketable job skills. But not all the homeless are so fortunate. Many cannot even read the classified ads in the newspaper. There are as many as twenty-five million people in the United States who cannot read. There appears to be a strong link between poverty and illiteracy. Illiterate adults earn 42 percent less than high school graduates.[7] Illiteracy isolates and handicaps adults who would like to lead successful lives. There are several organizations that teach adults to read and help them break out of poverty.

Reading Is Fundamental is a national organization that invites children to participate in their projects. (See Appendix I for address.)

Note to Parents and Teachers: A pictorial perspective of the homeless in America is available in most libraries and is a great discussion aid when teaching kids about poverty. It is called *American Refugees* by Jim Hubbard and is published by University of Minnesota Press in Minneapolis.

Projects for Kids to Help the Poor

Grade Level:	K -12
Skills Needed:	Varied
Time Required:	Varied

1. Start a Kids Care Club

You Can Help

There are many charity projects that kids can do alone, but it is more fun and more productive to work with others. A Kids Care Club can respond to the needs of the poor in your community and in the world. You can start a Club with a group of neighborhood kids, a school class, a church youth group, or a religious education class. Anywhere kids are working together to help others, there is a Kids Care Club in the making.

Here's How

Kids Care Clubs can meet around a kitchen table, in a basement, a parking lot, a school cafeteria, a church, or a classroom. In a pinch the Club can function without a formal meeting place, using phone messages and mailings to keep kids informed.

1. The first step is to plan your first project. A favorite first project is making bag lunches (Project 2). Participants can bring loaves of bread, and local markets can donate peanut butter, jelly, and fresh fruit. The kids can decorate the lunch bags with colorful pictures and happy messages. This is a fun project because it works for five or fifty kids, but any of the projects listed in this book could be used.

2. Invite kids to join your Club. The Independent Sector in Washington, D.C., did a study on teen volunteerism. They found that 86 percent of kids who were personally invited to volunteer said yes. In addition to asking your friends and family, you can also distribute flyers around school, put an advertisement in the local paper or school newsletter, hang post-

ers in local stores, and ask the principal to announce your project on the loudspeaker.

3. Keep track of the kids who come to each Club project by using a sign-in sheet (sample form in Appendix II). The sign-in sheet will become your membership list.

4. Register your Club with the National Kids Care Clubs and you will receive newsletters with ideas from other kids around the world. Just write a letter and explain why you want to help others. Send it to: Kids Care Clubs, P.O. Box 1083, New Canaan, CT 06840.

5. You can call meetings or remind the Kids Care Club members of an upcoming project by using a phone tree (each Club member is responsible for calling another) or mailing a Club newsletter.

6. After each project, write a short article for the local newspaper and list all the members who participated in the event. (Use the Publicity Worksheet in Appendix II.)

Grade Level:	K–12
Skills Needed:	Making Sandwiches
Time Required:	3 hours

2. Bag Lunches

You Can Help

Many soup kitchens serve only one meal each day. But one meal doesn't provide enough nutrition for a person to stay healthy. Some soup kitchens also distribute healthy bag lunches with the hot meal they serve each day. Homeless people can save the bag lunch for later in the day when they get hungry again.

Here's How

You or your family can make a few bag lunches for a soup kitchen, or you can get some friends and make many bag lunches. Bag lunches should contain a healthy sandwich, a piece of fresh fruit, cookies or some other treat, and a napkin. Most soup kitchens serve more than a hundred guests each day; many kitchens serve several hundred. Most soup kitchens would welcome your help with bag lunches.

1. The first step is to decide which soup kitchen you will distribute the bag lunches through. In Appendix I is a listing of state coalitions that serve homeless people. You can call the coalition in your state for a list of soup kitchens and homeless shelters in your area. If your state does not have a coalition, or if the coalition cannot help you, call your social welfare office and ask to be referred to a soup kitchen nearby.

2. Call the soup kitchens to find out if they would like your bag lunches, when they need them, and how many they could use. Schedule a date and time to deliver the lunches.

3. Make a list of the items you will need to make the lunches (foil, lunch bags, bread, peanut butter, jelly, cookies, fruit, napkins). Begin to solicit donations from family, friends, and local merchants.

4. Get other volunteers to help you make the lunches. Plan a time to make the lunches, allowing at least three hours before the soup kitchen expects you to deliver them. It takes less than thirty minutes for ten people to make a hundred bag lunches, but you have to allow for ''goof-off'' and travel time.

5. Transport the lunches to the soup kitchen. Depending on the number of bag lunches you make, you may need more than one car.

6. Perhaps you can stay at the soup kitchen and help hand out your bag lunches.

Note: It is especially fun to decorate the paper lunch bags. It takes more time to create colorful designs on each lunch bag, but the homeless people love it, especially the children. They know it took extra time for you to decorate each bag, and they appreciate that you cared enough about them to want to make them smile.

Grade Level:	K–12
Skills Needed:	None or gardening
Time Required:	3 months, part-time

3. Grow a Community Garden

You Can Help

In years past, most families had a garden in which they raised fresh produce for themselves and to share with neighbors. But many families today do not have access to land for gardening, and many children have never seen a real vegetable garden. Fresh produce is available in most parts of the United States, but it is often expensive. Fresh vegetables have become a luxury the poor can't often afford.

Here's How

You can grow a garden and share the produce with a poor family, a homeless shelter, or a soup kitchen.

1. Find a sunny location for your garden. It could be in your yard, or you could get permission from the city or town to use a park, or a parcel of school property. Make sure the garden is fifteen to twenty feet away from large trees or shrubs.

2. Prepare the soil by breaking it up with a shovel or a rototiller. This is the most important step in successful gar-

dening. Often the soil will need fertilizer or other treatments. Read books in your library about gardening to determine what your soil needs.

3. Plant the seed and keep out the weeds. The weeds eat the nutrients in the soil that the vegetables need to grow.

4. Decide who will receive your produce. Perhaps your pastor or priest knows of someone in need. If not, you can deliver the produce to a local shelter or soup kitchen and help prepare and serve it to homeless guests.

Note: This project can be expensive without donations from garden shops.

Grade Level:	2–12
Skills Needed:	None or cooking or serving plates
Time Required:	2–4 hours

4. *Help in a Soup Kitchen*

You Can Help

Soup kitchens serve free meals to anyone who is hungry. Usually soup kitchens are in churches, community centers, or part of a homeless shelter. For many homeless people, these kitchens provide their only source of nourishment each day. The name ''soup kitchen'' is misleading, because most soup kitchens serve many foods other than soup, and many soup kitchens don't even have a kitchen! Volunteers cook the meals in their own kitchens and transport the hot food to the soup kitchen.

Here's How

You can volunteer to cook food in your home and deliver it to a soup kitchen near you. Or you can volunteer to work at the soup kitchen serving the people who come there to eat.

1. Talk to the people who run the soup kitchens in your area. Ask them what they need. Do they need volunteers to bake desserts? Would they like you to make fresh salad one day? Could they use your help serving the food? What time do they serve? How many people eat there each day?

2. After you get feedback from the soup kitchen, pick a need you want to fill and make arrangements to do it. Perhaps you can enlist others to help with large cooking projects. (Many markets will donate food for use in a soup kitchen.)

Grade Level:	K–12
Skills Needed:	Collecting
Time Required:	2–10 hours

5. Basic Bags

You Can Help

Many homeless people don't have the basic tools they need to maintain their health. Even finding fresh water to brush your teeth is a problem when you live on the street. And how do you take a shower or wash your hair? Homeless shelters often have shower facilities for homeless people to use, but shelters need donations of toothbrushes and other basic supplies to provide for their guests.

Here's How

You can collect toothbrushes, toothpaste, small bars of soap, shampoo, combs, and washcloths to distribute to homeless people.

1. Ask your Kids Care Club, church, school, or neighborhood to help you collect basic hygiene items for homeless people.

2. Package the items in paper lunch bags (one toothbrush, one toothpaste, etc., per package). Decorate the bags with smiles and kind wishes.

3. Deliver the Basic Bags to a homeless shelter (or soup kitchen if no shelter is available).

4. Let the shelter know how to contact you when they use all the Basic Bags and need some more.

Grade Level:	K–12
Skills Needed:	Collecting Organizing
Time Required:	Varies

6. Canned Food Funds

You Can Help

Community food banks help supply soup kitchens with the food to prepare daily meals. Some food banks also fill grocery bags with canned food for families to take home with them. Soup kitchens have food pantries where families can get bags of canned food to take home. You can keep your community food bank or soup kitchen pantry supplied with canned goods, or you can start your own food bank. Kids in Santa Ana, California, started a food and clothing bank for students who needed help. They called the program SAVVY (Santa Ana Volunteer Youth).

Here's How

Ways to Collect Canned Food

- Sponsor a dance with canned food as the admission ticket
- Collect canned food door-to-door in your neighborhood
- Start a canned food drive at school, with classrooms competing to collect the most
- Place a bin in your local market, with posters asking for donations
- Call local churches and ask for their support
- Have a sidewalk fair with games, rides, and crafts. Instead of selling tickets for each event, require a certain number of cans or a certain type of canned food.
- Organize a Walk-A-Can. Solicit donations of a certain number of cans per mile you walk
- Ask grocers and food manufacturers to make donations
- Invite the local Boy Scouts or Girl Scouts to help

Where to Store Canned Foods

If you are supplying a community food bank, the food can be delivered to the existing facility. However, if you are starting a new food bank, you will need to find a suitable place to store the food that you collect. It is helpful to choose a storage site that is easily accessible to the people who will use the canned food. Some examples are a local church, a local soup kitchen, a school classroom, the community center, the welfare office building, or a low-income day-care center.

If you cannot locate space for storing your canned food in a public place, you can store canned foods in your basement or garage. (Bagged or boxed foods should not be stored in basements or garages, since they are more vulnerable to humidity and insects.) Once or twice each month, you can bag the canned food and take it to a distribution location.

Finding a Distribution Location

When food is stored in a public place, the distribution is very simple. Just use posters to let people know what days the food bank will be open to give away food. The food should be bagged prior to that day, if possible. When the food bank is open, you should supervise the distribution to be sure that no one takes more than his or her fair share.

If food is stored in your basement or another private location, you can load bags of canned food into a car and deliver them to a local soup kitchen, the welfare office, day-care center, school nurse's office.

Note: For safety's sake accept only labeled cans with legible expiration dates. Periodically check the dates on cans to be certain the contents are still safe to eat. Throw away cans with expired dates.

Carefully inspect bent or damaged cans for holes. When air gets into cans, the food spoils and is unsafe to eat.

Grade Level:	K–12
Skills Needed:	Baking
Time Required:	2–4 hours

7. Bean Bread

You Can Help

Homeless people and poor families may not get all the nutrition they need from one meal a day at the local soup kitchen. A small loaf of bread can supplement their nutrition, especially if the bread is made with whole grains and ground dried beans, which provide protein.

Here's How

Bean bread is not available in stores, so you will have to make it at home.

Kids Care Bean Bread Recipe

By Heather Spaide, 13 years old

1 cup white flour	¼ cup brown sugar
1 cup whole wheat flour	¼ cup molasses
½ cup bean flour	1 teaspoon salt
2 packages dry yeast	2 tablespoons margarine
1 ½ cups milk	⅓ cup oats
¼ cup cornmeal	

Using a coffee bean grinder or food mill, grind enough dry beans (navy, red kidney, or any combinations of dried beans) to make ½ cup of bean flour. Set the flour aside. Heat the milk in a saucepan with the salt, molasses, brown sugar, and margarine. Do not boil, just get the mixture hot enough to melt the margarine. In a separate bowl, stir together the yeast and the white flour. Using a mixer, blend the bean flour into the milk mixture, and begin adding the white flour and yeast, the whole wheat flour, the oats, and the cornmeal. Use a wooden spoon or your hands to finish mixing the ingredients together. Knead the dough until smooth and elastic. Shape the dough into one large loaf or three small loaves of bread. Place them in greased bread pans and let rise until they have doubled in size. Bake at 375 degrees for about 35 to 45 minutes.

Distribute bean bread to homeless or poor people through soup kitchens or homeless shelters.

Grade Level:	K–12
Skills Needed:	Cooking
Time Required:	2–6 hours

8. Holiday Meals

You Can Help

Holiday meals can be a fun and filling occasion for most of us. Thanksgiving turkeys, cranberry relish, fruit punch, pumpkin pie with whipped cream, and many other delights decorate our family tables. But imagine the holidays without all the festive fixings. For some families, holiday meals consist of a bowl of cereal or a cup of canned soup.

Here's How

You can plan, purchase, and prepare a holiday meal for a poor family in your community and deliver it the day before, or on the holiday.

1. Talk to the social welfare agent in your community and get the name of a poor family that would like a holiday meal delivered to them. Or you can help an ex-homeless family. Families who have recently been relocated from a homeless shelter to low-income housing are often fighting a tide of bills and fears at holiday time. You can get their names from a homeless shelter.

2. Call the family to find out how many you should cook for, and what they like and don't like to eat. Arrange a time to deliver your meal.

3. Plan and shop for a meal that is custom-made for the family you choose to help. Make sure you include things like a stick of butter, napkins, milk, dessert, and maybe some tea or coffee for mom and dad.

4. Deliver the meal to the family and wish them a happy holiday.

Note: On a larger scale this project can also be done for a family shelter, an AIDS facility, a nursing home, a halfway house, or for on-duty police officers or firefighters.

Grade Level:	K–12
Skills Needed:	Cooking
Time Required:	2–4 hours

9. *Stone Soup*

You Can Help

Soups can be a very nutritious and easy-to-serve meal. Soup kitchens and homeless shelters are often happy to receive donations of homemade soups for their guests. Homemade soup for a hundred or more guests is a big job for one person, but if you have ever read the children's book called *Stone Soup* by Marcia Brown,[8] you know about a great trick for making soup!

Here's How

In the book *Stone Soup,* three clever soldiers trick a community into making a wonderful soup by getting them all to put one thing in the pot. Your Kids Care Club, church, school, scout club, or sports team can work together to create a delicious and fun soup for homeless people.

1. Talk to a local soup kitchen about donating a pot of homemade soup. What day? What time? How many should it serve? Should it be delivered hot or can they warm it there?

2. Borrow a couple of large pots from the soup kitchen, your church, or your school.

3. Ask everyone in your group to bring a prepared vegetable (any kind they want) and a large can of chicken broth to a designated kitchen (at someone's home, church, school, etc.).

4. Put the broth and some water in the pots and bring it to a boil. Add the vegetables.

5. Boil until the vegetables are tender. Season with garlic, salt, and pepper.

6. Place pots of soup in large cardboard boxes and secure with rolled newspaper to keep them from jiggling.

7. Transport your stone soup to a soup kitchen and stay to help serve it to the guests.

Grade Level:	Preschool to adult
Skills Needed:	None
Time Required:	2 or more hours

10. Family to Family

You Can Help

Struggling families need many kinds of support. Some parents may need help with home bookkeeping. Single moms may need help with baby-sitting. Some families need furniture or clothing. Some parents and older teens need transportation to job interviews. Many school-age kids need help with homework. Some families just need to know that someone cares.

Here's How

Your family can adopt a needy family. You can spend time with the family, get to know them, and help them with their needs.

1. Find a family that you can adopt through your church, social welfare agency, or a homeless shelter that serves families. It is helpful to adopt a family with children that are younger than those in your family, so that outgrown clothing and toys can be passed on to them.

2. Contact the family and talk to them about developing a friendship with your family. Make sure that the conversation is not belittling or insulting to the needy family.

3. Arrange informal get-togethers with your family (a trip to the park, a cook-out, a quick visit, an event at your church or their church). Find out what the family needs and how you can help them.

4. Help the family to meet its own needs and encourage the family to reach new goals. Here are some of the things your family can do for, or with, your adopted family:

- Share meals and holiday celebrations
- Have birthday parties for the kids and give presents
- Share good books to read
- Take them grocery shopping or to buy household supplies
- Give them your outgrown clothing and toys

- Go on family day trips together

- Offer them your old dishes or pans you no longer use

- Pass on your old bedspreads and curtains as you get new ones

- Help them paint a room

- Help with baby-sitting

- Help the younger kids with homework

- Work with the parents to design a household budget

- Provide transportation to job interviews

Grade Level:	K–12
Skills Needed:	Collecting
Time Required:	3–6 hours

11. Fresh Start Kits

You Can Help

When a family moves into a homeless shelter, they are often forced to leave their housekeeping belongings behind. Eventually these families are relocated from the shelter into low-income housing. It is hard to make their new apartment a home without simple cleaning supplies, kitchen utensils, or furniture.

Here's How

You can collect housekeeping supplies and give them to newly relocated homeless families.

1. Ask your Kids Care Club, class, team, church group, or friends in your neighborhood to collect items like laundry soap, dish soap, washcloths, dishcloths, bar soap, shampoo, sheets, towels, pans, dishes, flatware, baking supplies, laundry baskets, spices, and anything else needed to make a house a home.

2. Arrange the supplies in laundry baskets.

3. Deliver the filled laundry baskets to homeless shelters. Ask them to give a basket to each family when they are relocated into a new home.

4. Perhaps you want to leave a phone number at the shelter so that you can be notified when they need more baskets.

Grade Level:	6–12
Skills Needed:	Computer
Time Required:	1 hour weekly or more

12. Teach Computer Skills

You Can Help

Computer literacy has become an important part of our business community. Most schools teach computer skills to their students because they recognize the value of computer skills in the job market. But many unemployed adults have not been trained to use a computer, and many young people from poor school districts are not given enough opportunity to practice on the computer and develop their job skills. The chances for these people to get a good job would increase tremendously if they learned to use computers.

Here's How

You can teach unemployed adults and underprivileged teenagers how to use a computer and therefore how to improve their future opportunities.

   1. You can find people who need your computer tutoring through inner-city high schools (especially night school for kids who dropped out of school), community centers, or homeless shelters where homeless moms and dads are desperately searching for ways to improve their ability to earn a living.

   2. Try to get permission from a local school, shelter, or volunteer organization to use their computer for your tutoring. Also, some businesses will allow you to use their computers for such a worthy cause.

   3. Keep it simple. Be careful to downplay the complication of using computers. Don't use computer slang or other lofty language, or your student will be too intimidated to learn. Just start with typing skills and work into use of simple programs.

   4. Read books on beginning computer training.

   5. Help your student relate his or her new skills to real life. For example, she could work on writing a resumé or preparing a college application. If your student is interested in sports, help him graph the season's scores or write a mock article about one of his favorite coaches.

   6. Most importantly, always encourage your student. It is humiliating enough to need free help; don't make your student more embarrassed by pointing out every mistake. A good rule to follow is, Every criticism should be preceded and followed by a compliment. Put one negative between two positives.

Grade Level:	10–12
Skills Needed:	Wisdom and safety awareness
Time Required:	4–6 hours

13. Relief Trips to Homeless Areas

You Can Help

Some homeless people will not go into shelters or soup kitchens to get the food and supplies they need. Some are afraid of being attacked, and others have become too despondent to ask for help. These people are without food, water, shelter, blankets, and other necessities.

Here's How

You can collect food, bottled water, plastic raingear, and blankets to be delivered to the most needy homeless people.

1. Ask your Kids Care Club, school, church group, sports team, neighbors, or friends to collect fresh foods that do not need cooking (breads, fruit, etc.), bottled water, blankets, and raingear or sheets of plastic.

2. Call the police station in your community or a nearby metropolitan area to find out where homeless people stay. Ask the police to escort you to distribute your items.

3. The police may also be able to advise you on the best time to make your delivery. A group of teens from New York make relief trips to Central Park in New York City at midnight once a month.

4. Wear name tags with first names only. For the homeless, being able to call you by name will give them a sense of being connected and send the message that you recognize them as fellow human beings.

Note: One adult should be present for every three or four teens. Teens should be told to stay together and not wander away from the group. Homeless people can become agitated, so remind teens to ignore instead of engaging anyone who seems angry. Cameras may not be welcome. Ask permission before taking photos.

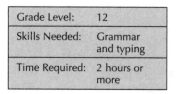

Grade Level:	12
Skills Needed:	Grammar and typing
Time Required:	2 hours or more

14. Write a Resumé

You Can Help

Most homeless people are also jobless. Many have marketable job skills but do not have the resources to sell their skills in the job market.

Here's How

You can help a jobless person sell his or her marketable skills and get a job.

1. Read a book on creating a good resumé. Ask people you know to let you see their resumés as examples.

2. Talk to a homeless shelter, unemployment office worker, or social welfare agent about helping unemployed people develop good resumés. Ask that someone be recommended for you to help.

3. When you find a person to help, find out everything you can about his or her work experiences, classes, work-

shops, volunteer jobs, hobbies, and interests. Help highlight his or her strengths and skills.

4. The resumé can either be typed by the jobless person, or you can take the information home to type it.

5. The best resumé is only paper unless it is mailed to prospective employers. Help the jobless person determine possible jobs and identify likely employers. Call the potential employer to get the name of the person who does the hiring. Mail the resumé to a specific person at the place of business.

6. Suggest to the jobless person that he or she make a follow-up call to the prospective employers a few days after mailing them a resumé.

Grade Level:	3–12
Skills Needed:	Cutting
Time Required:	2–6 hours

15. Design and Make Raingear

You Can Help

Only about one half of all homeless people spend the night in shelters. Many homeless people sleep on benches, under bushes, or in other makeshift homes. Even those who sleep in warm shelters at night are put back on the street during the day, regardless of the weather.

Here's How

You can make simple and inexpensive rain ponchos for homeless people. The ponchos should be lightweight and fold into a small package.

1. Purchase lightweight sheet plastic (about two square yards per poncho). You can find sheet plastic in hardware stores, some fabric stores, and many department stores. Make sure the plastic is not too thin, or it will be dangerous for young children who can suffocate if plastic gets caught on their faces.

2. Measure and cut the sheet plastic according to the sketch below, or design your own raingear. Perhaps you would like to make a couple of different sizes. A sheet of plastic cut two yards by two yards would make a good size poncho for a teenager or a small woman. Large men and women may need a poncho that is cut three yards by three yards. Experiment and see what you think.

3. Fold the raingear into a resealable plastic bag and label it with the size and name of your rain poncho. (You can give your design a more creative name than "Rain Poncho.")

4. Distribute your raingear through homeless shelters, soup kitchens, police officers who are in contact with home-less people, or social welfare workers. You could also visit a park where the homeless are known to sleep, and distribute them yourself.

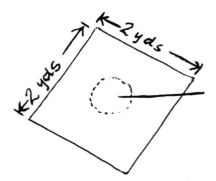

Cut a 12" to 18" hole in center of plastic.

Grade Level:	K–12
Skills Needed:	Coloring, cutting
Time Required:	½ hour to 2 hours

16. Promise Placemats

You Can Help

Many people are depressed because of the circumstances of their lives. Some have AIDS and live with the fear of dying. Some are homeless and live with the fear of living always in poverty. Some are fighting drug and alcohol addictions and live with constant confusion. Even when we can provide food and shelter and basic care for these people, how can we let them know we care about them?

Here's How

One way to send a message of care and hope is to make colorful placemats that will inspire and encourage the people who use them. A placemat is especially effective because it is used every day during mealtime.

1. Purchase fourteen-inch-long paper (it can be construction paper or just white copy paper) and a roll of clear contact paper (found in hardware and dime stores).

2. Make up some inspiring sayings, or use scriptures or quotes from famous people. Here are a few sayings you can use to get you started:

- You Are Tomorrow's Promise
- Love Begins Within You
- Dare to Care

• Dance With the Rainbows

• You Can Do It

• Give Love, Know Love, Live Love

3. Write a saying on the paper and create a colorful picture or design to illustrate the saying you choose.

4. Cut the clear Contact Paper the same width as the paper plus one inch, and twice the length of the paper plus one inch. (Example: If the paper is fourteen inches long and eight and one-half inches wide, you would cut the clear Contact Paper twenty-nine inches long and nine and one-half inches wide.)

5. Peel off the protective backing on the contact paper and center the decorated paper over the left half.

6. Affix the decorated paper to the clear Contact Paper carefully, leaving a one-half-inch margin. Fold the second half of the contact paper over the back of the decorated paper, making a complete seal all around.

7. Trim off the excess Contact Paper.

8. Give the placemats to anyone who needs a lift, or to children living in a homeless shelter, AIDS facility, or hospital. If you are ambitious, you could make enough for a family shelter or a soup kitchen.

Grade Level:	K–12
Skills Needed:	Hosting a party
Time Required:	4 hours

17. *Wish List Party*

You Can Help

Homeless shelters, soup kitchens, hospices, and AIDS facilities usually have a wish list which identifies all the items they need to keep their program running. Most lists contain small items, large items, and volunteer needs.

Here's How

You can ask for a wish list from a homeless shelter or soup kitchen and have a party to collect many of the items on the list.

1. Call a homeless shelter or soup kitchen and request a copy of their wish list.

2. Plan a party and design invitations which include a copy of the wish list. Ask people to bring items from the wish list instead of gifts.

3. Collect the wish list items at your party and deliver them to the shelter or kitchen. Take your friends along if possible.

CHAPTER 6

Responding to the Children

Charity's Child

There once was born a child who could not sleep. Day by day, his tiny body became weaker, until his tears were all that moved in his cradle. Though many doctors examined him, they could find no reason for the infant to remain awake.

"The child shall die of exhaustion before he is six months old," predicted the nurse.

In great despair, the father called a group of experts from around the world to cure the child. They could not agree on the cause or cure of the infant's suffering.

"The child needs a new organ," said the surgeon. "Let us operate to cure him."

"The child has a chemical imbalance," said the psychiatrist. "Let us prescribe a drug to cure him."

"The child is overstimulated," said the psychologist. "Let us change his environment."

"The child is an unusual case," said the researcher. "Let us study him."

Each expert wanted to prove his own theory about the child's illness. The surgeon went off to schedule surgery. The psychiatrist hurried to develop a new drug. The psychologist searched for a quiet room to move the child to. The researcher gathered pads and monitors for his study.

And the infant cried on.

But then, while the nurse was away on her rounds, a young boy passed by the nursery. Hearing the faint sound of suffering, he entered the nursery and saw the infant. Unaware of the complicated tangle of tubes that surrounded the infant, the boy reached into the cradle and lifted him to his chest.

"Don't cry," said the boy, "I will stay with you." So he held the infant and sang to him with whispered lullabies. The infant relaxed into the warm and comforting arms of the boy and became lost in the echo of his soothing songs.

When the nurse returned from her rounds, she found the infant sleeping peacefully.

"It's a miracle!" she gasped. And it was. It was the miracle of charity's child; of the caring instinct of a child who couldn't see the complications, only the suffering.

Understanding the Needs of Children

The largest section of this book is devoted to children because kids are naturally attracted to helping other children. Thirty-nine thousand children die in the United States each year before their first birthday,[9] many as a result of poor nutrition or lack of basic care. Five and a half million children go to sleep hungry each night in the United States alone,[10] many, many more worldwide. And more than 200,000 children are believed to be homeless[11] in our land of abundance.

Even when minimal food and shelter are provided, homeless and poor children are often disadvantaged by the environment they live in. They may have to play with broken or discarded toys. While the lack of toys may not be life threatening, toys do make important contributions to a child's development. Some toys teach

counting concepts; others teach cause-and-effect relationships.
Young children learn about the world through play. Consider what
the young child who plays with a rusty tin can is learning about
his world. It's a dismal lesson, isn't it?

For too many children, academic development is sacrificed to
the business of survival. Many homeless families are mobile,
making it difficult to keep track of school records and making
registration in a new school frustrating. These kids are embarrassed by their lack of proper clothing or school supplies, and
they fear the ridicule of other children. Many mornings they leave
home hungry and ill-prepared for the school day. They are frequently behind in their studies and need extra help from teachers
or the special education staff. Many kids drop out of school because they are convinced by life's tough lessons that they will
never be able to finish anyway. Some of the kids who drop out
find opportunities to make a living by selling drugs; others get
pregnant and start the cycle of poverty all over again.

Simple advantages like computers and other academic aids
may not be readily available for kids who live in poverty-stricken
areas. Many go home to empty apartments or houses and are responsible for themselves and often younger siblings until Mom
or Dad comes home from work. There are many things that we
can do to help these children.

Projects for Kids to
Help the Children

Grade Level:	K–12
Skills Needed:	Crafts
Time Required:	Varied

18. Kid-Made Toys

You Can Help

You can provide educational toys for young children who cannot afford their own. There are many books in the library about making toys from wood or cloth, or games you can make with paper and markers.

Here's How

1. Whatever toys you choose to make, be sure that you give away only safe toys, without sharp edges, toxic paint, splinters, loose parts, or exposed nails.

2. You can deliver the toys to a family homeless shelter.

3. You can entrust a social welfare worker to distribute them to families on welfare.

4. You can take them to a low-income day-care center.

5. You can leave them at a hospital for sick children to play with.

6. You can leave them at a soup kitchen for the homeless kids who eat there.

7. Following are some inexpensive ways to make toys:

Nature's Toys

Nature provides many toys for free. Acorns and glue can become wonderful pictures or creations. Corncobs can be turned into cute little dolls with dried husks for hair. Twigs and branches are as good as pick-up sticks. Pinecones are fun to decorate, toss, hide, or string together. Dried flowers make pretty pictures. Sand has been a favorite plaything since beaches were created.

Recycled Toys

Recycling toys makes less waste for the environment to absorb, and makes a young child happy. Clean up old toys that are hanging around in the closet, and ask your friends to do the same.

Other throwaway materials can be used as toys. Plastic containers can become a child's play dish set. Brightly colored pictures from magazines can be glued to index cards to make fun flashcards for kids. Old socks, when filled with dry beans, make great beanbags. Old socks can also be transformed into puppets with buttons for eyes. With a little imagination, boxes can be turned into play stoves, refrigerators, or castles.

Blocks

Among the easiest, safest, and most educational toys to make are building blocks. Just ask the lumberyard to cut a two-by-four or two-by-two into small pieces, and sand them well. You can paint them if you want to, but it isn't necessary. Building blocks provide hours of creative fun for young kids (even older kids like them).

Play Dough

Play dough is more than fun, it is therapeutic. Psychologists believe that kneading and pounding on play dough can relieve tension and help kids deal with stress. Play dough is easy to make and, stored properly, will provide weeks of fun for children. Just mix three cups of flour with one cup of salt. Add one-fifth cup of vegetable oil and only enough water to make a stiff dough. Color with food coloring and store in airtight containers. If the dough sticks to your finger, mix in a little more flour.

Finger Paints

Also therapeutic is finger painting. Finger paints can be made by mixing powdered paint with soap flakes and liquid starch. Edible finger paints can be made from instant pudding.

Flannel Board

Flannel boards are a great way to play alone or in a group. Individual boards can be made with an eight-by-ten-inch cardboard backing, covered tightly with flannel fabric which can be secured with masking tape on the back. Figures of animals, trees, flowers, and people can be cut out of colored felt.

Giant Bubble Fun

Kids love to make bubbles. It is especially fun (and educational) to make large bubbles with various objects. Make the bubble solution by mixing one part dish soap with three parts water. Strings tied in circles and hangers bent to make large ovals produce great bubbles.

Bean Bags

Tossing bean bags is a game most of our grandparents played. Old socks or mittens are easily filled three-quarters full with dry beans, and the opening is sewn shut. The bean bags can be tossed into trash cans, buckets, pots, or even plastic jars.

Grade Level:	2–12
Skills Needed:	Telephone calling Transporta-tion
Time Required:	1–5 hours a month

19. Reading Robin Hood

You Can Help

Riding a bike is good leg exercise. Reading a book is good brain exercise. Even very young children are stimulated by the colors and pictures in books. But some children have many books and some children have none.

Like Robin Hood, you can take from the rich and give to the poor. (Unlike Robin Hood, you should ask permission before taking books.) Many families would love to get rid of some of the children's books they no longer read. Some people would be happy to donate new books to kids who need them. Publishers, bookstores, libraries, and schools are all sources for you to ask for books to give away to kids who don't have books of their own.

Here's How

You and your friends can collect books from those who have many, and distribute them to needy children without any. There are many ways to get the books, and many children who need them. Here are a few ideas to get you started.

1. You can collect books for deprived children by:

- Putting a donation bin in your local bookstore and making a poster asking patrons to buy a new children's book and donate it to underprivileged kids

- Writing letters to publishers of children's books (you can get their addresses from *The Writer's Digest*) and asking for donations of their slow-selling books. Remind them of what great publicity it will be for them!

- Canvassing your community for secondhand children's books and asking your friends to join the effort and canvas their neighborhoods, too

- Asking your school superintendent to give you the old textbooks from primary grades

2. Where you can take the books you collect:

- Donate them to a local homeless shelter. Tell the shelter supervisor to let the kids each keep one or two and to call you when they need more.

- Start a Robin Hood Mobile. Take your collection of books to low-income day-care centers, homeless shelters, local parks, and public housing developments to give them away.

- Mail a package of books each month to the children in a local struggling family. The kids will love getting a package in the mail, and you can send the books anonymously.

- Ask your Social Welfare Department to help you distribute the books to needy families

3. If you would like to do more than collect and give away books, you can use the books you collect to help a child learn to read, or learn to love to read. Reading Is Fundamental is an organization that encourages literacy (the ability to read) through schools and volunteers. Inspired by many boys and girls who were happy for the opportunity to share their reading skills with younger kids, Reading Is Fundamental started a new program called Leaders for Literacy. Leaders for Lit-

eracy invites middle and high school kids to work with younger children in schools or homeless shelters to teach and encourage reading skills. The older kids run the program, think of motivational activities or games, and choose the books for the younger kids to read. Not only does this program help young children love to read, but it also puts young children in contact with teenagers who are helping others. What great lessons in human kindness and literacy the older kids are teaching! (See Appendix I for address.)

Grade Level:	2–12
Skills Needed:	Reading
Time Required:	1 hour to unlimited

20. Read to a Sick Child

You Can Help

Minutes seem like hours to a child who is sick and lying in a hospital bed. Maybe he misses his own bed, or riding his bike, or even going to school with his friends. Maybe he is a little scared about all the things that the doctors and nurses are saying to him. Maybe he just wants to get up and go home. But he can't. You can't help a child go home from the hospital any faster, but you can make the time he is there go by faster.

Here's How

1. You can visit a sick child in the hospital and read your favorite stories to him or her.

2. Make sure to choose books that the child will understand, and try to choose books that tell a funny story.

3. When you are reading the story to the sick child, keep these things in mind:

- Always get permission from the nurse before reading to a sick child

- Be sure to show the sick child any pictures on each page

- Read slowly and pronounce the words clearly

- Add drama whenever you can. For example, if the man in the story shouts at a dog, raise your own voice to read that part. It is also fun to change your voice to sound like a woman, or a child, or a man when those characters appear in the story

- If you plan to read to the same child again, find out what books and subjects the child would like to hear

- If you can, leave the book with the child to look at until the next time you come

- When time allows, bring paper and crayons to make a picture of the story with the child

4. If you would like to do this project with a group of your friends, there are some ways to make it more fun for everyone. For example, you can read the book like a skit. Each one of you can take the part of one or more characters in the story and act out the story as you read it. Maybe you can even go to the hospital dressed in funny costumes that look like the characters in the book. This project works great when there is a ward full of children who would all like to hear the story.

5. Another fun reading activity that would invite the participation of the young patients is to read the first part of the story and then let the sick children write their own endings. You and your friends could act out each ending as the children wrote it. The children will love watching their own endings

being acted out before their eyes. Later, tell the children the actual ending of the story as the book tells it. But assure them that their endings were better.

Grade Level:	6–12
Skills Needed:	Teaching
Time Required:	1–5 hours

21. Teach a Disadvantaged Child

You Can Help

A disadvantaged child is any child who must overcome a struggle before he or she can grow up healthy, educated, and happy. The struggle could be a physical or mental handicap, it could be poor nutrition that interferes with the ability to learn, or it could be poverty that robs the child of opportunities to develop his or her own special talents.

But the saddest disadvantage is an emotional one. The emotionally disadvantaged child is the child who thinks he or she is not worth our extra effort, the child who gives up early and trips into the future without any hope of fulfillment. There are too many of these disadvantaged children in our world. But you can help them discover their own worth and develop their own strengths.

Here's How

You can volunteer to help children who are disadvantaged by handicaps, learning disabilities, poverty, or poor self-esteem within your own school district.

1. You can teach a disadvantaged child a sport or a special skill like typing or playing a musical instrument, or help with homework. What you teach isn't as important as the message you give by taking the time to be with him or her. You are saying that you think he or she is worth your energy and time. Here are some things you can teach a disadvantaged child:

- How to do homework

- How to study for a test

- How to use a computer

- How to play basketball, soccer, or football

- How to dance ballet or jazz

- How to play chess

- How to play a musical instrument

- How to start a Kids Care Club

- How to sew

- How to cook

- How to make things from wood

- How to paint

- How to plant a garden

- How to baby-sit

- How to find what you want at the library

2. Use your imagination. There are many things you can do that a younger child would like to learn from you.

3. You can find children who need your help by talking with your principal or guidance counselor. If they can't help you find someone, call the principals of the elementary schools in your area. You can also talk to the director at the

local Head Start program for preschool children, or the YMCA or YWCA.

4. If you would like to work with handicapped children, there may be special schools that teach handicapped kids in your area; these are listed in the Yellow Pages of your phone book under ''Schools.''

Grade Level:	K–12
Skills Needed:	None
Time Required:	25 minutes to unlimited

22. Be a Friend to a Friendless Kid

You Can Help

Imagine what it might feel like to be friendless. Perhaps you move to a new school and don't know anyone. Perhaps your closest friend just moved away, and now you don't have anyone to hang around with. Perhaps you know lots of people, but no one knows you because you are too shy to make friends. Or perhaps people just aren't nice to you because you are different. It isn't much fun to be all alone when others are having fun with their friends. It is even worse if the other kids are picking on you because you are different from them. No human being deserves to be lonely.

Here's How

You can be a friend to someone who is lonely. This is more a project of opportunity than of planning. You will know when someone needs your friendship, and you can be ready to respond. Here are a few simple rules for being a friend:

1. Make the person feel as though you want to be his or her friend, not as though you are just being friendly as an act of charity.

2. Remember that a friendless person may have some rough traits, since he or she may not have had a lot of practice at friendship. Give him or her plenty of time to learn to trust you.

3. Develop an equal relationship, with both of you sharing ideas and making contributions to the friendship. Don't try to do all the giving.

4. For older kids, be careful when starting a friendship with someone of the opposite sex. As innocent as you may intend the relationship to be, he or she may get the wrong idea and get hurt instead of helped. Be very honest from the start.

5. Don't try to change your new friend by suggesting new makeup or an updated wardrobe. Just accept who that person is and find things you admire.

6. Defend your new friend if others try to make fun of him or her.

7. Don't ignore the things that make your friend different; talk about these things when they come up.

8. Don't come on too strong. Just be around when your friend needs you.

9. Keep your friend's secrets.

10. If you discover that your new friend has some problems that are too big for you, seek the help of a trusted adult.

Being a friend isn't always easy, and you might not be successful every time you try. But it is worth the gamble if the friendship works out. I'm sure it is worth the effort, because twenty years ago I met one of my two best friends when she moved to our high school and didn't know anyone. She is still one of my favorite people and closest friends.

Grade Level:	2–12
Skills Needed:	Writing
Time Required:	1 hour

23. Homeless Pen Pal

You Can Help

Don't you like to receive letters? Most of us like to receive letters because it lets us know that someone was thinking about us. But some kids never receive any mail; they don't have a home to send it to. They don't have next-door neighbors to recognize them and wave to on the street. They don't have a telephone to call their family, and they don't have a car to take them for a visit with their friends. These people, often runaway teens, feel disconnected with their past, their families, and their communities. The friends they make in the homeless shelters and soup kitchens last for a while, but many of their homeless friends will find a job and move on to another area. Something as simple as a letter can help a homeless person feel less alone.

Here's How

You can become a pen pal to a homeless teen and give him or her a new connection to the community. You don't have to write long letters or say anything special, just a simple letter about yourself and a few questions for your pen pal to answer. It is nice to find a pen pal that has things in common with you, such as someone who is your age and likes a similar sport. But it can also be wonderful to choose a pen pal who is completely different from you, such as someone who is younger than you and lives in another state. You can learn a lot about life from people who are different from you.

    1. When considering the kind of pen pal you would like

to find, you should think about how close (in distance) you would like your pen pal to be. If you think you might like to meet your pen pal in person and maybe spend some time together one day, then you should choose a pen pal in your own area. If you like the idea of learning new things about different cultures, you can choose a pen pal who lives in a different part of the country or world. Many people prefer distant pen pals who they will never meet, because they feel more comfortable telling their pen pal all the things they can't say to people they see every day. Also, many homeless people feel hostile to the communities they are living in, for not helping them more. If you write to a pen pal from another area, it might be easier for him or her to talk to you about the frustrations of being homeless.

2. After you have narrowed the field to a specific age group and area, you can make some calls to homeless shelters to get a name for your pen pal. (See Appendix I for a state-by-state listing of homeless shelter coalitions you can call.)

3. Ask the director of the shelter to connect you with a homeless person in the age group, and with the interests that you describe.

4. If the director thinks someone at the shelter may be interested, offer to call back the next day for the name and address. The director will have to ask the homeless person if he or she would like to receive letters from you. Don't ask the director of the shelter to call you back if you are calling long distance; every dollar is needed to help the people who live there.

5. When you write to your pen pal, try to include a photo and lots of information about youself. Here are some things you might want to include in the first letter you write to your pen pal. Don't use them all, just choose a few to write about.

About Yourself

- Your age and grade, what you look like, and things about you that describe who you are

- Your brothers' and sisters' names and ages

- Your favorite sports or activities

- The weather in your area (if your pen pal lives far away)

- How you feel about school, and your favorite (or least favorite) subject

- Something that your favorite (or least favorite) teacher did recently

- Your friends' names and what they are like

- Something you wish you could do better, or recently failed to do right. (This will make your pen pal feel more comfortable with you because you admit that you make mistakes too.)

About Your Pen Pal

- What grade is he in?

- Does he like school?

- How many brothers and sisters does he have?

- What does he like to do after school?

- What is his best friend's name? What is he like?

- What does he want to do during the summer?

- What is his favorite food?

- What is his favorite sports team?

- Who is his favorite singer?

*What **Not** to Say*

- Don't talk about all your new toys or computer games; he may not have any
- Don't talk about your bedroom or spend much time describing your home; remember, he doesn't have a bedroom or a home
- Don't ask too many questions about the shelter; he may be embarrassed
- Don't say anything about feeling sorry for him
- Don't tell him about you recent vacation to Disneyland
- Don't make promises you can't keep (such as "Maybe my dad can get your dad a job")

Basic Letter Format:

Date

Dear Pen Pal [use name],

    My name is......[finish letter]

Your pen pal and friend,
[sign your name here]

A word to parents: Most homeless people are nice folk who are out of work or low on luck, but some are drug addicted and desperate for funds to support their habit. Ask the director at the shelter to give you the name of someone who will respond to your child's friendship appropriately. But be aware that even with the recommendation of the shelter director, you could get a pen pal who tries to take advantage of your friendship by asking for money, difficult favors, or perhaps even showing up at your door for shelter. If the possibility of these events makes you uncomfortable, you may want to focus on a pen pal in a different state or country.

Grade Level:	4–12
Skills Needed:	Transportation Various housekeeping skills
Time Required:	1–3 hours

24. Single Parent's Helper

You Can Help

Many children are growing up in homes with only one parent instead of two. Single parents have all the work of two parents: a full time job, the laundry, the shopping, the cleaning, the home repairs, the PTA, the doctor appointments, and all the other cares of day-to-day survival. Often these unending chores rob the parent of sleep and leave the parent feeling frustrated and lonely.

Here's How

You can help a single parent with some of the many jobs he or she must do. You probably already know a single parent that you would like to help (perhaps your own home is run by a single parent).

1. If you don't know a single parent who needs some help, ask your pastor, the school nurse, or the director at a local day-care center to suggest someone.

2. Here are some things you can do to help:

• Perform light housecleaning chores (vacuum, dust, or water plants)

• Deliver a fully cooked dinner to their home

• If you drive, offer to pick up groceries or do an errand

• Walk the dog or give him a bath

• Wash the car

• Shovel snow from the walkways in the winter

• Mow the lawn during the summer

• Stack firewood

• Help with simple home repairs (fixing a broken step, etc.)

• Clip coupons for weekly shopping

• Baby-sit while Mom or Dad takes a break

• Ask. The parent may need something that isn't on this list

Grade Level:	K–12
Skills Needed:	Writing Repairing Classifying
Time Required:	3–20 hours start-up

25. Toy Library

You Can Help

For many families, toys are a luxury they can't afford. They must spend any money they earn on rent and food; sometimes they can't afford even these. Toys are the last things on their shopping list. But young children don't just like to play with toys, they *need* to play with toys. Toys teach young children about their world, about language, about early math skills, about cause and effect, and toys allow children to develop their minds and their creativity. Children need toys.

Here's How

You can give young children access to a wide variety of toys that are educational and fun. You can start a toy library where parents can bring their children to ''check out'' a toy, just as you might ''check out'' a book at the school library. The children would be allowed to keep the toy for two weeks, then return it and get another toy.

1. Start by collecting new and gently used educational toys for children from one to twelve years old.

2. You can write an article for the newspaper asking the community to make donations, or you can start a toy drive in your school. Area merchants may be willing to donate some toys too.

3. Make sure that the toys are safe for young children (see the section entitled Safe and Responsible Toys below) and not easy to break.

4. The toy library can be located in your school, in a local day-care center, in the local book library, in the social welfare offices, at a pediatrician's office, or in a van that travels around once a week making routine stops.

5. With a permanent marker, put a number on each toy you collect. For each toy, you will need a large index card. Write the toy's number on the upper left-hand corner of the index card, then write the description of the toy on the right-hand corner.

6. Each time a child "checks out" a toy, you will write the borrower's name, phone number, and due date on the index card.

7. Here are some ways to let families know about your toy library:

- Send a flyer home with the children in elementary schools

- Send a flyer home with the children in day-care centers

- Write an article for your local newspaper

- Put up posters in your library, grocery store, doctor's office, and social welfare department

8. Unfortunately, some people may try to take advantage of your good will by stealing the toys. There are some things you can do to prevent theft, but nothing is foolproof. You should keep track of the borrower's name, address, phone number, name and address of their employer, and the names of two local relatives or friends. This way, if they fail to return a toy in the future, you have a list of people you can call to get the toy back. Also, people are less likely to steal something if they know you have the phone number of their employer and their relatives.

9. You could also charge a five dollar membership fee, one time only or once every year, for the privilege of using the toy library. The five dollar fee is not much money, but it is enough to make parents feel invested in your program and not want to jeopardize their ability to take full advantage of their membership. The money you make from the fee could be used to replace broken toys or buy new ones.

10. The toy library would probably be open only once a week for a couple of hours. The big job is getting it started, which could take many hours. After the library is up and

running, you will need to open it only once a week, call bor-
rowers who are late returning toys, and repair any toys that
are returned broken.

Safe and Responsible Toys

Although there are many toys on the market today, some are
not safe or appropriate for young children. You can ask an
early childhood professional (like the director at a licensed
day-care center) to help you select the toys. When selecting
toys for the toy library, make sure to keep the following
points in mind:

- Avoid sharp edges, glass parts, and rough, splintery
  wood
- Make sure any paint is nontoxic and not chipping
  off
- Remove any plastic coverings that might get into
  the hands of little children
- Do not accept toy guns, knives, or other violence-
  promoting toys
- Do not accept toy characters that dismember
- Electrical toys are hazardous for unsupervised
  young children
- Toys that use batteries will be costly to keep
  running
- Try to choose toys that teach something or allow
  creative thought
- Make sure age requirements are clearly labeled on
  the toys (a toy for an eight-year-old should not be
  lent to a two-year-old child)

Grade Level:	8–12
Skills Needed:	Writing Researching Speaking
Time Required:	3 hours

26. Child Safety Advocate

You Can Help

Mrs. Lorenzo wiped her tears with the back of her hand as she waited outside the emergency room for her husband. Her long dark hair was twisted to one side to hide the tangles that she hadn't time to comb out. Her wrinkled blue coat hung open in the front, revealing the pink nightgown she hadn't had time to change out of. How would she tell her husband the news? How could she even say the words? Why did this happen to their baby? Could she have prevented it? How could she have known that the paint on their apartment walls had lead in it? How could she have stopped little Jeremy from putting pieces in his mouth every now and again? Babies do that, they put everything in their mouths. But now their two-year-old baby was fighting for his life, and even if he lived, he would probably be brain damaged. Why?

Samantha walked to school every day from her suburban home. Her blond curly hair bounced as she walked. She was always smiling. One time she walked into the school doors by accident. It must have hurt. She didn't even frown, just smiled and kept walking. She had a reputation of being accident prone. Not many of her friends ever saw her accidents, but she often came to school with bruises and once even with a broken arm. One day she wasn't in school. The principal announced that she had been in an accident and was in very serious condition at the hospital. We found out later that her stepfather had been arrested for beating her. Why?

A large mall in Connecticut decided to put a merry-go-round in the upstairs food court to attract children. Next to the merry-go-round was an iron fence that went around a large hole in the floor where a circular stairway dropped to the first floor. Very pretty. Carefully placed next to the iron fence was a bench. I watched as one child after another came over to the bench to watch the merry-go-round. But you know how kids are on benches. They stand up, they look over the back, they dance, they rock. They do anything except sit down. After one child almost fell over the back of the bench and down the one-story drop to the first floor, I asked the management to move the bench away from the fence. The management said the bench looked nice there and no one had fallen yet.

Seven-year-old Joseph lives with his mother and his five sisters in a one-room apartment. They have no electricity, no heat, and no working toilet.

Eleven-year-old Sally is ''on duty'' at three o'clock. She must walk her younger brother and sister home from school and baby-sit until her mom gets home at six.

Every day millions of children are injured, abused, ignored, and neglected. They suffer quietly because they don't know that they have any rights. They depend on others to take care of them. But sometimes that system breaks down, and the people who should care for them don't, or can't. What can children do when the people they depend on are unable to keep them safe?

Here's How

You can give the children a voice. You can remind the world that children have the right to a safe environment. And you can teach the children that they are important members of our society, worthy of our attention and protection.

1. The first step is to focus on a specific problem and research the facts. For example, if you choose to represent abused children, you can write to all the organizations that help abused kids and ask them to send you information.

2. It would also be helpful to talk to victims of abuse.

3. Here are some of the other problems affecting our children:

- Neglect of physical needs (food, heat, water, hygiene)

- Emotional abuse (being told they are stupid or ugly)

- Runaways (often leaving an abusive home)

- Lead poisoning from old paint

- Unsafe halls and stairways in apartment buildings

- Exposed electrical outlets in apartment buildings and public places

- Conditions that expose children to unnecessary risk (the bench at the mall)

- Unpaid child support (leaving kids to suffer poverty)

4. Once you have focused on a problem and gathered the facts about the problem, you can begin speaking for the children.

5. You can put attractive posters with your message around town, write an article for the paper, leave stacks of flyers at grocery stores, send flyers to local radio or TV stations, and offer to discuss the problem further on the air.

6. You can prepare a skit or musical concert about the problem and offer to perform it for your school, church, or other organization.

7. You can organize a fund-raiser to benefit the children you are advocating. (See Chapter 10, Fund Raisers.)

Grade Level:	7-12
Skills Needed:	Arts and crafts
Time Required:	2 hours weekly

27. *Therapy for Abused Children*

You Can Help

Abused children often lock their feelings inside. Sometimes they don't even remember being abused. Perhaps their mind is trying to protect them from the harsh truth. But feelings that are held prisoner in a child's mind won't sit quietly for long. They will find a different way out. Sometimes sad feelings will make a child depressed, and he or she just gives up on life. Sometimes hurt feelings make a child angry, and he or she gets into trouble a lot. Sometimes fearful feelings make a child physically sick.

Here's How

The best way for children to get control of their feelings is to learn how to name them. Art is a natural and nonthreatening way for children to express their feelings. You can give abused children the opportunity to learn about their feelings through simple art projects.

1. Parents Anonymous is an international self-help organization for adults who are abusive to their children. The meetings are typically once a week for ninety minutes to two hours. The parents bring their children with them. Parents Anonymous is always looking for volunteers to watch the children during the meetings, so the adults can discuss better parenting skills without disruption. You can volunteer to watch the children.

2. Plan an art project for each week. The art should not be too instructed, since you want the children to express themselves and not just follow directions. Blank paper, paint brushes, markers, or crayons are all you need to bring. Here are some things you can ask the children to draw:

- A picture of yourself
- A picture of how you feel tonight
- A picture of God
- A picture of something that makes you happy
- A picture of something that makes you sad
- A funny picture
- A scary picture
- Your favorite pet
- A picture of a sunny day
- A picture of your home

3. After the children have made their pictures, give each child a chance to talk about what they drew and why.

4. Try to use the pictures to help the children develop a "feelings vocabulary."

5. Write each new feeling in a notebook, and ask all the kids to contribute to the definition of the feeling. Also, use the pictures to teach the children to accept their own feelings and the feelings of others.

6. If there is not a Parents Anonymous group meeting in your area, or if you are not interested in making a weekly commitment, you can volunteer to hold a feelings workshop for children in a local day-care center. One in every ten children is abused, so in almost any classroom, you will be working with one or two abused children without knowing who they are.

Grade Level:	4–12
Skills Needed:	Cleaning Repairing
Time Required:	3–9 hours

28. Repair a Day Care

You Can Help

Millions of young children spend five days a week, nine to ten hours each day, in a day-care center. Most day-care centers are happy places, where children can play, learn new things, make lots of friends, eat good meals, and are safe while Mom is away at work. But day care is a tough business. Insurance is too high, teacher salaries are too low, and parents cannot afford to pay what it costs to keep the center running. Many day-care centers turn to the government for subsidies and grants. Other centers just struggle along, with old toys and torn books, until the state shuts them down, leaving children with no place to go.

Here's How

You can help a day-care center provide the best possible environment for the children who stay there.

1. You can mend torn books, repair worn playground equipment, fix broken toys, wash grubby easels, launder splattered smocks, sort mixed-up puzzle pieces, plant flowers or replant grass in bare spots, clean windows, copy worksheets, mend doll clothes, freshen the rabbit cage, disinfect the teething toys, file paperwork—the list is endless.

2. Just call or write to the nonprofit day-care centers in your area with your offer to help. List all of the things you would be willing to do.

Grade Level:	K–12
Skills Needed:	Bagging
Time Required:	2 hours

29. Bag a Snack

You Can Help

Imagine what it would be like to be a child living in a homeless shelter. One child who visited a homeless shelter thought it wouldn't be so bad; after all, there were always lots of other kids around to play with. But what about inviting classmates over after school? Or having a birthday party? Or changing the channel on the television? Or taking your time in the bath? Or just leaving your school bag on the kitchen table? Or calling a friend on the phone? Or opening the refrigerator to get a little bedtime snack? Would you miss any of these things?

Young children have smaller stomachs than adults do. They need to eat more often. In some shelters the evening meal is served at 4:00 P.M., leaving too many hours until the next meal at break-fast. Lots of homeless children go to bed hungry every night.

Here's How

You can make bedtime snacks for kids who live in homeless shelters.

1. Choose healthy snacks that will keep without refrigeration for a day or two. Here are some snack ideas:

- Cookies and a tangerine

- Nuts and raisins and a boxed juice

- Crackers and raisins

- Apple and American cheese

- Bagel and boxed juice

- Corn muffin and boxed juice

- Pretzels and a peach

- Carrot sticks, cookies, and boxed juice

2. Find a homeless shelter that houses families with children (use Appendix I or call the local Social Welfare Department). Call the shelter and talk to the director about bringing some bagged bedtime snacks. Find out how many children live there and what kind of snacks they like.

3. Arrange for a day when you can drop off your bagged snacks and get a tour of the shelter.

4. Put the bedtime snacks in individual paper bags.

5. Decorate the bags if time allows. You can make enough snacks for just one night, or for many nights. After you pack the snack bags, put them carefully in a box and deliver them to the shelter. Be sure to pack a few extra bags in case new children move into the shelter before you deliver the snacks.

Avoid plastic bags because of the suffocation danger to young children. Also avoid sugary snacks since the children will be going to bed soon after eating them.

As an added treat, you can write a short, happy bedtime story (be sensitive to your audience) and photocopy it to put in all the bags. Or you can deliver your bagged snack during the evening and read the children a bedtime story. Maybe you will even have enough time to play some games with them.

Note: This project is similar to Project 2, Bag Lunches. You can review Project 2 for further information or ideas.

Grade Level:	5–12
Skills Needed:	Phone answering
Time Required:	1 hour a day or week

30. Latchkey Call-In

You Can Help

A latchkey child is a child who comes home from school to an empty house or apartment. Some children are home alone for several hours before Mom or Dad returns from work. Latchkey kids fix their own snacks, and often dinner too. Sometimes latchkey kids get scared being alone. They might be approached by a stranger and not know what to do. They might lose the electricity and be afraid of the dark. They might try to cook something and get burned. Or they might just wish someone would help them with their homework.

Here's How

You can start a call-in program for latchkey kids. The kids would keep a special latchkey number by their phone and be able to call with concerns or problems. You could answer the phone and help them decide what to do.

1. If there is a group of kids doing this project, you can ask the school to let you use one of their phone numbers. It wouldn't be used as a latchkey line until after school, so it wouldn't interfere with school business.

2. Every weekday, after school, one of you would be ''on duty'' to take calls from latchkey kids. You could stay at the school to answer the calls (and do homework in between calls), or you could have the calls forwarded to your home. (Check with the phone company about call forwarding in your area.)

3. Beyond taking calls from worried latchkey kids, you could also make a list of kids who go home alone, and call them to make sure they get home okay. If you make this list, be sure it is kept confidential, since it would be dangerous if the wrong person got a list of where vulnerable children lived.

4. The project can be expanded to include handing out bags with a healthy snack and a fun project for the latchkey kids to do after school. The call-in number should be printed boldly on the bags.

Note: The best solution to the latchkey problem is an after-school program for latchkey kids. You can encourage your community to provide this service for the children, and then you can volunteer to help with the kids.

Grade Level:	2–12
Skills Needed:	Repairing Painting Washing
Time Required:	3–6 hours

31. Adopt a Worn-out Playground

You Can Help

Playgrounds are magical places for kids. They provide a safe environment for children to exercise their bodies and their imaginations. Even in the busy cities, where backyards are uncommon, playgrounds provide children with a world of nature and new experiences. For many city children, the playground may be their only source of outdoor recreation. Unfortunately, many playgrounds have been worn down by weather and abuse, and town or city budgets just don't see them as a priority.

Here's How

1. You can find a worn-out playground and adopt it.

2. Make a list of the repairs the playground needs and improvements you would like to make to the playground.

3. Find out who owns the property, and send them a letter like the one below.

4. Ask local stores to donate the things you need to repair the playground.

5. Get a group of friends to help with the project.

Date

Dear Sir,

We are a group of concerned citizens who would like to improve our local parks. We have identified the park at [give address of park] as one we would like to work on. We have listed the repairs and improvements we would like to make at no cost to you. Please write to us with your permission for this work.

Suggested repairs and improvements for the park at (give address of park):

- Sand and paint the jungle gym
- Pick up litter and rake land
- Wash picnic tables

We will try to complete all repairs during one Saturday. We will schedule the repairs as soon as we receive your letter of approval. Thank you for providing a safe place for our children to play.

Sincerely,

(Your name, address and phone number)

Grade Level:	7–12
Skills Needed:	Writing Phoning
Time Required:	3–9 hours

32. Turn Trash Into Treasure

You Can Help

This project combines caring for our planet with caring for its people. Every day, America alone throws away one million tons of trash. You can imagine what the world total might be. Industry contributes greatly to the trash problem by throwing away dump trucks full of scraps and waste materials. Many of the products that industry discards could be useful to homeless shelters, schools, and day-care centers, but the companies can't afford the time to find out who needs them.

Here's How

In Portland, Maine, the Creative Resource Center operates a shop for teachers and parents of young children which sells industrial "trash." Paper of all sizes, leather scraps, buttons, scrap fabric, spools, film containers, laces, and many other treasures are on sale for pennies. The shop is a well-known resource for schools and day-care centers. You may not want to open a shop, but you can be the middleman between the industry and the kids.

1. You can contact companies about turning some of their waste products into treasures for small children. Here are some of the treasures that companies can provide:

- Film shops have plastic film containers that kids can store little treats in
- Wallpaper companies have outdated sample books that make great book covers or art projects

- Carpet companies have carpet scraps and samples that kids can use to sit on at school

- Carpenters have wood scraps that can be sanded and turned into blocks for kids to build with

- Electrical supply companies have empty wooden spools that wire comes on, which can be painted and turned into little round tables for kids

- Paper companies have miscut or discontinued paper that day-care centers and schools can use for art projects and writing

- Shoe manufacturers have leather scraps and laces that kids can use for various projects

- Clothing manufacturers have buttons and fabric scraps that kids can use for art and sewing fun

2. After compiling a list of treasure trash that is available in your area, you can call or write to homeless shelters and day-care centers in your area to let them know where these products can be found.

Grade Level:	5–12
Skills Needed:	Repairing
Time Required:	2–20 hours

33. Recycled Bicycles

You Can Help

The previous project was about finding useful ways to recycle our trash. This project is similar, but specifically about bikes.

Thousands of bikes are thrown away each year. Many have busted tires or broken brakes, and some are just too small or outdated for the owners. But for every bike that is thrown away, there is a child somewhere who would love to be riding it. In some parts of the world, biking is a major form of transportation. Adults use them to go to work and to do their shopping, and children use them to get to school and visit their friends.

Here's How

Justin Lebo found a broken bike when he was ten years old. He decided to rebuild it and give it away. He worked in his garage. He had so much fun with this project that he began looking for other bikes to rebuild. He successfully rebuilt and gave away more than seventy bikes over the next three years.

1. Like Justin, you can set up a bike repair shop in your garage, basement, backyard, school, or at a local service station.

2. You can find discarded bikes at dumps or through people who know what you are doing, and transform them into working bikes for children who can't buy bikes of their own. Some of the old bikes can be used for spare parts, and others can be repaired to working condition.

3. How to find old bikes:

- Search the dump
- Ask trash collectors to hold them for you
- Put a public service announcement in the newspaper (usually free)
- Write an article for the newspaper
- Put public service announcements on the radio
- Put up posters asking for old bikes in bike stores and schools

4. Where to find kids who need recycled bikes:

- Call counselors at elementary schools

- Write to your Social Welfare Department, or Family and Children's Services

- Ask the director of a homeless shelter

- Ask local pastors and religious leaders

Grade Level:	9–12
Skills Needed:	Writing
Time Required:	1 hour every month

34. Pen Pal Detention Centers

You Can Help

Kids who have committed a crime are sent to a place called a youth detention center. The centers are more like strict schools than prisons, and the kids are there to learn to be better citizens. Many of the kids in youth detention centers are victims of abuse. All of them deserve a second chance to make a contribution to their world. Imagine how it would feel to be locked away from your home, your family, and your friends. Imagine how it feels to wonder if your family and society will ever forgive you for your crime and accept you. Imagine how it feels to believe that you are just basically bad.

The children who live in youth detention centers are full of fears and doubts. Many act tough, but it's just a mask to hide how afraid they really are. While they are in the detention center, they may learn math and spelling, and they may even learn how to respect our laws, but how will they learn to like themselves again?

Here's How

You can help a young person who is trying to start over. You can begin a writing friendship with a kid in a detention center that offers him or her support and assurance that the world doesn't hold a grudge. The content of the letter is not important. It is the contact with someone outside of the detention center that will heal weak self-esteem and quiet debasing doubts.

1. You can get the name of someone to write to by calling the Department of Corrections in your state and getting the number for the youth detention program.

2. When you call the youth detention center, ask for the chaplain or the psychologist on the staff. They are interested in the emotional and spiritual well-being of the children who live there and should be happy to help you.

Grade Level:	9–12
Skills Needed:	Baby-sitting
Time Required:	2–12 hours

35. Operation Graduate

You Can Help

Every fifth baby today is born to a teenage girl. Life is tough for a teen mom, who is little more than a child herself. A baby can mean the end of her social life and her education. Without an education, how will the young mom support her child? More than half of the teenage moms in America get stuck on a long-term lifestyle of welfare. They give up their hopes and dreams for the future to raise their babies and settle for a life of state-supported poverty.

Here's How

You can help a teenage mom complete her education and pursue her dreams.

1. You can baby-sit for her child while she attends night courses at the local high school or community college.

2. You can also offer to help her study for her tests. It is always easier to learn when someone is helping you, quizzing you.

3. If you would like to help more than one mom finish her education, you could approach a school where night courses are held about letting you use a classroom to baby-sit several children while their moms are taking courses.

4. Perhaps the best way to open the doors for teenage moms to finish school, and teach young people how to care for children at the same time (a skill that every teenager should be taught), would be to have a day-care center in the local high school. Teenage moms could leave their children at the day-care center while they attended classes with their friends. Students who are interested in young children could register for a class in early childhood education, which would include an hour of student teaching in the day care center each day, as well as learning from lectures and textbooks.

5. You can introduce the idea of a day care center in your high school to your superintendent of schools or school board. Try writing to the superintendent first; if you don't get a positive response, take it to the community at large by writing a letter to the editor of your newspaper. Send the same letter to every member of your school board. Ask friends to write letters to the editor, too.

Grade Level:	K–12
Skills Needed:	None
Time Required:	1–3 hours

36. Holiday Kits

You Can Help

Young children love to make their own valentines, decorate their own Easter baskets, and make their own Christmas cookies. And what mother wouldn't prefer a handmade Mother's Day gift to a store-bought present? Every holiday offers children the opportunity to stretch their imaginations and exercise their creativity. Creativity is not only fun for children (and adults too), but it is also an outlet for stress and a healer of low self-esteem. However, many children do not have access to the art materials necessary for even the simplest holiday project.

Here's How

You can put together holiday kits that include everything a young child would need to stimulate his or her creativity.

1. Holiday kits can be packaged in shoe boxes, grocery bags, or just tied together with newspaper and a string.

2. You can make holiday kits with a specific project in mind (like a painted flower pot for Mother's Day), with easy-to-read instructions inside, or the kits can be open-ended, with only the child's imagination to direct him.

3. The kits can include any of the following arts and crafts materials:

- A small bottle of glue or glue stick
- Scotch tape
- A box of crayons or markers

- Construction paper
- White paper
- Blunt-tipped scissors
- Fabric scraps (you can include needle and thread for older kids)
- Stickers
- Stencils
- Artificial flowers
- Ruler
- Pages from old magazines with colorful pictures
- Colorful wallpaper samples
- Lace paper dollies
- Envelopes
- Colored pasta
- Colored rice (dry rice mixed with a drop of food coloring)
- Pipe cleaners
- Cotton balls
- Pine cones, acorns, colored leaves
- Tissue paper
- Tracing paper
- Modeling clay
- White paper plates
- Nontoxic paints and brush

4. The supplies that you include in the kits will vary depending on the project, the holiday season, and the age of the children you are making the kits for.

5. You can deliver your kits to children who live in a homeless shelter or a low-income day-care center.

6. It would be really fun if you could stick around after you deliver the kits to help the children make things with them.

Grade Level:	5–12
Skills Needed:	None
Time Required:	1–3 hours

37. Rock-a-Bye Baby

You Can Help

Thousands of infants spend nine to ten hours each day in day care while their moms and dads try to earn enough money to provide them with food and clothing. Most day-care centers are safe, warm, and caring places where all the physical needs of the children are attended to. But when two teachers have eight babies to care for, they may not get much time for cuddling each child. Cuddling may not seem like a basic need, but for little babies, rocking and cuddling are as urgent to their well-being as food and shelter. Many babies spend too much time lying alone in cribs or sitting alone in infant seats. By the time Mom arrives to pick up her baby, the baby is determined to have her full attention. Unfortunately, working moms also have to attend to dinner, laundry, cleaning, and other household chores. So baby gets put alone in another crib or infant seat.

Here's How

You can help a little baby get some of the attention he craves by volunteering in a low-income infant day-care center.

1. You can call day-care centers that accept babies and volunteer to come to the center and spend time rocking the babies. Maybe you could volunteer one hour a week, or whenever you have some time to spare after school. Remember that day-care centers are typically open from 7 A.M. until about 6 P.M. every weekday. The last two hours of the day

are hardest on the babies and the staff, so it is an especially good time to have energetic volunteers show up.

2. Be sure that you are very clear with the teachers at the day-care center that you are volunteering to rock babies, not clean floors or run errands.

3. The name of this project is Rock-a-Bye Baby. However, I would not suggest that any baby should have to hear the old version of that lullaby:

> *Rock-a-bye baby on the treetop.*
> *When the wind blows, the cradle will rock.*
> *When the bough breaks, the cradle will fall,*
> *And down will come baby, cradle, and all.*

Who told us this lullaby was comforting to young children? Try singing a new version to the babies you rock, like this one or something you make up on your own:

> *Rock-a-bye baby on the treetop.*
> *When the wind blows, the cradle will rock.*
> *When the birds sing, the baby will sigh,*
> *And baby will slumber till morning is nigh.*

Grade Level:	K–12
Skills Needed:	Repairing Carpentry
Time Required:	1–3 hours

38. Toy Carts for Hospitalized Children

You Can Help

Children who are hospitalized experience a lot of different feelings. They may be scared by the loud noises and high-tech machines. They may be worried and confused about what's happening inside their bodies. They may be annoyed at all the shots and prodding. And, if they have been in the hospital for many days, they may be bored stiff with the soap operas and *Lassie* reruns on daytime television. Pediatric departments try to keep toys, books, and games around for kids to play with, but they need constant repairing and replacing. Busy nurses don't have time to go toy shopping every week.

Here's How

You can help children who are in the hospital feel a little better by repairing and replacing the worn-out toys, games, and books. In some hospitals the toys are kept in a special playroom, and the children go to the playroom when they want to play. In other hospitals, the toys are kept on a rolling cart which is pushed from one room to another, and children choose a toy or book to keep in their room. Some hospitals have a playroom for the mobile children, and a playcart to take to the rooms of the children who cannot leave their beds.

1. You can visit your hospital pediatric department and find out what toys they already have for the children and what toys they would like to have. You can also make a list of the toys or books that should be repaired, and what supplies you will need to repair them (for example, glue, masking tape, sandpaper, etc.) and plan to return with the supplies.

2. If your hospital does not have a rolling toy cart for bedridden children, perhaps you can volunteer to design and build one for them. Basically it would be similar to a small bookcase on wheels, only the shelves should be wide enough to hold games and toys.

3. You can check on the toy supply at the pediatric department every couple of weeks to see if they need any new toys or repairs. When many children are using the same toys,

it doesn't take long for paper supplies to dwindle, paints to run dry, puzzle pieces to get lost, pages of books to get torn, pencils to need sharpening, and play dough to crumble.

4. One pediatric nurse requested ''project kits'' that she could take out for the children on special days. For example, if a project kit contained everything ten children need to make salt dough sculptures, the nurse could pull out the kit whenever she had extra time and the young patients were bored. Any arts or crafts project can become a kit, and nurses would probably like to have several choices. You can use your imagination in designing project kits, but here are the ingredients necessary for a Salt Dough Sculpture Kit for ten children:

5 cups of salt	Nontoxic paints
5 cups of flour	10 paint brushes
Wax paper	Spray can of polyurethane
Large plastic container	Roll of paper towels

Instructions for making salt dough sculptures

The instructions would tell the nurse that the salt and flour should be mixed with enough water to make a play-dough-consistency material. The children could shape the dough into any number of things. In the spring the dough could bloom into beautiful flowers, at Valentine's Day the dough could become little or big hearts, at Christmas the dough could make homemade tree ornaments, and of course the children could make animals or other forms any time of the year. After the children mold their dough, it can be baked slowly in the oven at 300 degrees, or sun-dried in the children's hospital room windows. After the sculptures are dry, the children can paint them with the nontoxic paints, and later the nurse can spray them with polyurethane to preserve and protect them.

Grade Level:	K–12
Skills Needed:	Collecting
Time Required:	1–6 hours

39. Baby Layettes

You Can Help

Every mother wants to take good care of her newborn baby. She wants to dress her baby in warm clothes, give him or her good food to eat, soft blankets to snuggle in, a sturdy crib to sleep in, and clean diapers when the need arises. But the fact is that many babies go home from the hospital to a chilly home, empty cabinets, a dresser drawer for a crib, and threadbare blankets to keep them warm. Some babies stay in wet diapers until their bottoms bleed from rashes and chapping. Some babies sleep in rickety old cribs with slats that are so far apart that the baby could get his or her neck caught during the night. One in every five young children goes to bed hungry in the United States; the ratio is much higher in other parts of the world. It is not that the mother and father don't want more for their baby, but they don't have more to give.

Here's How

You can put together a baby layette to send home with a needy new mother.

1. The kit can include any combination of baby items such as:

Bottles	Pacifiers
Formula	Juices
Cereals	Baby foods
Diapers	Rubber pants
T-shirts	Baby lotion
Baby shampoo	Baby soap

Baby oil	Teething rings
One-piece pajamas	Washcloths
Sweaters	Hats
Baby booties	Crib sheets
Receiving blankets	Tissues
Crib blankets	Rash ointments

And how about some flowers for Mom?

2. You can pack the kit in a small plastic laundry basket, a grocery bag, an infant seat, or a new or slightly used diaper bag.

3. Distribute the kits through your local hospital. Ask for permission to give the kit to the new mom yourself, and maybe you'll get to see the new baby, too!

Grade Level:	K–12
Skills Needed:	Collecting
Time Required:	2–12 hours

40. First-Day-of-School Bags

You Can Help

For young children, there are not many days as exciting as the first day of school. Unfortunately, for some kids it is also a day of humiliation. While their friends are unpacking their brightly colored book bags, full of crayons, pencils, glue, and such, these children sit quietly in their seats, stuffing the brown bag with one pencil and a sandwich deep into the cold desk in front of them. These kids can't afford the luxury of school supplies; they must rely on what the school is able to provide for them.

Here's How

You can fill the first day of school with happy memories for a needy child. You can make First-Day-of-School Bags for children who can't buy their own. You can also give the bags to children in homeless shelters.

1. Collect book bags that are new or used.

2. Fill the book bags with school supplies that are appropriate for the age of the children you will give them to. (Ask a teacher to help you make a list.)

3. You can ask local businesses to contribute supplies.

4. You can sponsor a fund-raiser and buy the supplies.

5. You can start a school supply drive in your school or church. Or you can just ask neighbors and friends.

6. The bags can be distributed by social workers or a homeless shelter for needy families, or you can leave the bags with the principal of an elementary school and ask her or him to distribute them secretly on the first morning of school.

Grade Level:	10–12
Skills Needed:	Phoning Driving
Time Required:	1–3 hours

41. Unborn Care

You Can Help

Millions of babies are born each year with low birth weight because their mothers did not get proper prenatal care. Low birth weight in newborns translates into an increased risk of infection, learning disorders, slowed physical development, and a higher chance of sudden infant death.

Programs exist to help mothers get the proper prenatal care they need, but many mothers don't know about the programs or

are hampered by lack of transportation, depression, or just forgetfulness.

Here's How

You can help an unborn child enter this world with a healthy head
start. To help the baby, you will have to help the mother.

- You can help prenatal clinics call pregnant mothers to
  remind them to come in for their check-ups

- You can call a pregnant mother and make sure she is
  taking her vitamins every day and that she has all the
  healthy food she needs to eat

- You can invite a pregnant mother and father over to
  your home for Sunday dinner, or take a basket of
  healthy foods to them to eat

- You can pick up the phone and encourage a mother
  with drug, tobacco, or alcohol problems to make it
  through one more day of abstinence

- You can collect used maternity clothes for her to wear

- You can give her a warm comforter to help her sleep
  well at night

- You can take her shopping for groceries

- You can give her rides to her doctor appointments

- You can just be her friend

- You and your family can decide to adopt a single
  mother-to-be and invite her to share your home and
  hot meals while she is waiting for her baby to arrive

Grade Level:	K–12
Skills Needed:	Collecting
Time Required:	1–8 hours

42. Children Without Childhood

You Can Help

Kris followed the nurse through the dingy halls of the Albanian hospital. She walked slowly past the children missing an arm or a leg and the children with bandaged faces and bruises over most of their bodies. Many were little children, two to a crib, with injuries caused by a hateful war. There were no toys in their cribs, no mobiles dancing in the air, no colorful pictures on the wall. Everything was painted in a once-white, chipped gray.

Kris reached into her pocketbook and pulled out a worn teddy bear that belonged to her son. She held it out to a five-year-old boy with leg braces and large brown eyes. He took the bear with two fingers. Holding it beyond his face, he studied it first this way and then that way. Then he gave it back. Kris didn't know what to do. She put the bear under her chin and hugged it. The little boy smiled. Now he understood. He had never before seen a teddy bear nor any other toy at all.

Many child victims of war, famine, and poverty in the world have never seen a toy. The children who are lucky enough to survive to recuperate in a hospital must just lie in bed for hours every day. Toys won't solve the life-threatening problems they face each day, but toys can warm their hearts and encourage their minds to wonder while they recover from their injuries.

Here's How

You can give a little childhood to children who are growing old too fast.

1. Collect small toys and stuffed animals to send to children in desolated areas. Here are some ideas for collecting toys:

- Have a toy drive in your school, church, or community

- Ask toy stores or toy manufacturers to make donations

- Hold a fund-raiser and use the money you earn to buy toys

- Ask your high school or middle school to have a dance or a sports event with an admission fee of one or two small toys

2. You will find that collecting the toys will be the easy part. The harder part is getting the toys into the hands of children who need them. Unless you own an airline, you will probably have to rely on others to distribute the toys for you. Americares is a Connecticut-based charity that ships medical and humanitarian supplies to many devastated areas of the world. They will often include a box or two of small lightweight toys in some of their shipments to hospitals or orphanages. (See Appendix I for their address.) Other large international charities may also be happy to accept any toys you collect and distribute them to very needy children around the world.

Grade Level:	2–12
Skills Needed:	Fund-raising Writing
Time Required:	1–3 hours

43. Send a Child to School in Tanzania

You Can Help

In many countries, an education is available to every child. But in some countries, there is no formal public education. There are no schoolhouses, no books, no teachers, nor bells at recess (sounds great to some kids). Studies show that societies without a viable education system suffer devastating effects. The people fail to learn to read or write, so communication is difficult. Alcoholism increases in proportion to the poverty and hopelessness of life. Crime becomes a mode of survival, and immorality produces many orphaned children.

For the children of Tanzania, the only hope of learning is through a private education system which costs ten dollars a year (and that includes fabric for their school clothes). But the ten-dollar tuition may as well be ten thousand dollars for some families who don't have any money at all. They just cannot afford to send their children to school.

Here's How

You can help a child in Tanzania go to school next year.

1. Do some chores to earn the ten-dollar tuition and send it to the Maryknoll Fathers in New York. (They run the schools in Tanzania; their address is listed in Appendix I.)

2. Write a letter to Father LeJacq in Tanzania and tell him that you sent money to Maryknoll for a child's tuition,

and you would like him to arrange for that child to be your pen pal. His address is:

> Father Peter LeJacq
> c/o Maryknoll Fathers
> Bugando
> PO Box 1421
> Mwanza, Tanzania

3. If you don't hear from Father LeJacq within a couple months, you should write again. The mail may have been lost on the way to his home.

4. Don't send or request photographs from your Tanzanian pen pal; they are superstitious about pictures.

5. This project can be used with children in other unschooled areas. Tanzania is the area for which I have the addresses and contacts. You may find others through international organizations that help children, or through the United Nations.

Grade Level:	K–12
Skills Needed:	Drawing Sewing
Time Required:	1–3 hours

44. My Little Pillow

You Can Help

Little children with cancer and other serious illnesses often spend long periods of time in hospitals away from home. Sometimes their moms and dads can't even be with them. It can be very lonely and scary to be a little boy or girl in a big busy place without Mom or Dad around. And to make matters worse, the children are sick; some won't get better. Nurses try to make the children comfortable, but they can't be with them every minute.

Here's How

You can make a snugly little buddy that will stay near a sick child all the time: a cheerful little pillow.

1. Just use permanent colored markers, fabric paint, or cloth stencils to make a picture on a small pillowcase or a piece of fabric that can be stitched into a small pillow.

2. Stuff the pillow casing with nonallergenic polyfill and sew the end closed.

3. If you live close to a hospital that cares for children with cancer and other serious illnesses, you can deliver the pillows to the children in the hospital yourself.

4. Try to spend some time reading to or playing games with the kids.

5. A variation of this project is to take plain pillows and fabric paint with you to the hospital and let the children help make their own pillows.

6. If you don't live near a hospital for children, you can pack the pillows in a box and mail them to a hospital like St. Jude's Hospital for children. Put a letter in the box explaining what the pillows are for and giving your address in case any of the children would like to write to you.

Grade Level:	K–12
Skills Needed:	Collecting Organizing Asking
Time Required:	2–4 hours

45. Bear Hugs

You Can Help

Recently, while traveling in Richmond, Virginia, I saw a plea on the local cable television channel for teddy bears. Paula Hersh, the promoting manager at Continental Cablevision of Virginia, calls the program Great Bears for Kids in Danger. People in the community are asked to donate new or slightly used teddy bears to comfort children in emergency situations. One little girl who saw the appeal for bears ran to her toy box and pulled out all the teddy bears she could find. Her mother used the opportunity to discuss the benefits of sharing. "The Great Bears program provides comfort for the kids who receive the bears, but it is also a great teaching tool for children who give the bears," said Ms. Hersh. The bears are collected by the Richmond Police Department and given away to young children who are injured or traumatized in accidents. The children can keep the bears after the emergency is over. A little bear may not sound very important to older kids or adults, but to a very young child a cuddly bear sends a message of safety and calm, which is exactly what any child in an emergency situation needs to feel.

Here's How

You can help children in emergency situations who are hurt and scared by sending them a bear hug.

    1. Contact your local police department or hospital emergency room and propose the Bear Hug project to them. If they

are interested in giving new teddy bears to injured children, ask for the number of children they typically serve over a three- or six-month period. That number is your bear goal.

2. Get your friends or Kids Care Club to start a teddy bear drive.

3. Ask stores to participate in the drive by:

• Contributing bears

• Allowing you to leave a box in their store for contributions

• Agreeing to match the number of bears that customers donate in their store

• Allowing you to put a poster in their window

4. Ask your school and church to participate in the drive. Put boxes for donations in the lobby and hang posters in the lobby and halls.

5. Ask the community to contribute to your bear drive also:

• Put an announcement on the radio local stations

• Send flyers to news channels, newspapers, and cable TV

• Hang posters all around town

6. Collect the teddy bears and deliver them to the police department or the emergency room.

7. Ask for a tour while you are there.

CHAPTER 7

Responding to the Elderly

A Letter From President Reagan About Growing Older

My Fellow Americans,

I have recently been told that I am one of the millions of Americans who will be afflicted with Alzheimer's disease. . . .

At the moment I feel just fine. I intend to live the remainder of the years God gives me on this earth doing the things I have always done. I will continue to share life's journey with my beloved Nancy and my family. I plan to enjoy the great outdoors and stay in touch with my friends and supporters.

Unfortunately, as Alzheimer's disease progresses, the family often bears a heavy burden. I only wish there was some way I could spare Nancy from this painful experience. When the time comes I am confident that with your help she will face it with faith and courage.

In closing let me thank you, the American people, for giving me the great honor of allowing me to serve as your President. When the Lord calls me home, whenever that may be, I will leave with the greatest love for this country of ours and eternal optimism for its future.

I now begin the journey that will lead me into the sunset of my life. I know that for America there will always be a bright dawn ahead.

Thank you, my friends. May God always bless you.

Sincerely,

Ronald Reagan

Understanding the Needs of the Elderly

Former President Reagan wrote this letter on November 15, 1994, at the age of eighty-three. He had just been diagnosed with a disabling illness called Alzheimer's disease. It causes forgetfulness, confusion, irritability, weakness, and reduced verbal involvement with family and friends. Alzheimer's disease affects one in every three elderly people in America.

My grandmother, Mamie, was eighty-six years old when she wrote a book of family stories for her great-grandchildren. She is now a peppy ninety-year-old who is fortunate to enjoy good health. Her memories of another

> *Don't regret growing older,*
> *It is a privilege denied to*
> *many.*
> FROM A BIRTHDAY CARD

time, courageous people, and a different way of life have always been important to our family. More than important, her memories are the legs of our family, the part that makes us all one, holds us together, and carries us into the future.

The elderly are grouped together by age, yet they are unique individuals who have lived different experiences and learned different skills. They have felt the excitement of new life coming into the world, they have felt the grief of losing loved ones and old friends, they have been hurt by people and by illness, but they have survived. They would love to share their experience and their wisdom with us; in fact, they are desperate to share it with us. If youth can find something useful in their past, then their old age can find new meaning.

In some societies the elderly were exalted as religious leaders, medicine men and women, great sages, teachers, and prophets. Their experienced wisdom was respected, and their place in the community was urgently important. But modern society, in its frenzied search for eternal youth, has deflated the contributions that the elderly can make. We have found places to keep them "out of the way" where they will be safe but not an inconvenience for our fast-paced world. We treat the elderly with a quiet condescension called ageism.

Ageism is the youthful attitude that says, "Move over, old man, and let the stronger, faster man take care of things." Ageism is forced retirement and forced idleness. Ageism is the car horn that blares when an old woman is driving too slowly on the highway. Ageism is the young woman who complains that social security comes out of her paycheck. Ageism is youthful repulsion at wrinkles, false teeth, dribbles at dinner, hearing aids, bent backs, crooked fingers, and repetitious stories. For the elderly, ageism leads to the loss of self-respect, the loss of usefulness, and the loss of human dignity.

Consider the physical course of the elderly. The first hint of age may be an increased susceptibility to illness and disease. Then the senses may begin to rebel. Perhaps the eyes don't focus well, or the ears don't hear conversations in the same room, or the sense of taste dulls and food loses its appeal, and even touch may not produce the pleasure it once did. Later, the muscles may become weak and shaky, causing things to be accidentally dropped and even an occasional fall. The bones are more brittle, so falls often result in hospital visits to repair broken arms or hips. Broken bones take longer to heal, because the blood circulation is not as competent as it once was. Just walking up a flight of stairs is more difficult, with a respiratory system that is working retirement hours. And perhaps worst of all, the memory may

Thelma B. Weymouth entertains her seven great grandchildren.

begin to fail, and threats of mental incompetence whisper ever closer.

Now consider the emotional and social course of the elderly in our society. Many are forced to retire before they are ready. Without a regular paycheck, they will depend on pensions and social security to survive. Some will experience a 50 percent drop in income at this point.[12] Often that means moving from the home where they raised their children into a small apartment or some other less expensive housing. They leave behind friends and neighbors, not to mention all the coworkers that retirement claimed. What's left? Well, for the lucky, they still have their children and grandchildren to interact with. But in our transient world, their children may live miles or even countries away, and the interaction may be reduced to a Christmas visit once a year.

Many elderly are utterly isolated. This isolation has been referred to as "disengaging" from society, and some believe the elderly themselves are partially to blame. They are depressed by their inability to contribute to a society that places value on production. They see themselves as useless. They are convinced that

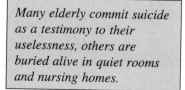

Many elderly commit suicide as a testimony to their uselessness, others are buried alive in quiet rooms and nursing homes.

old age is a burden, an embarrassment. Many elderly commit suicide as a testimony to their uselessness; others are buried alive in quiet rooms and nursing homes. Is this the lesson we want our children to learn about growing old?

Dr. Paul Tournier, in his book *Learning to Grow Old,* said, "We have given things priority over persons, we have built a civilization based on things rather than on persons. Old people are discounted because they are purely and simply persons, whose only value is as persons, and not as producers anymore."[13]

The elderly need to feel needed, useful, wanted, and loved. Behind that wrinkled smile and those cloudy eyes is a mind full of memories, experiences, wisdom, feelings, and ideas. The elderly see more than they did when they were younger, not with their eyes but with their hearts.

The following activities are intended to do more than provide a few services for the elderly; they are intended to integrate the elderly back into our world. Every project that brings the youth of today in touch with the elderly of today will restore dignity and hope to both generations.

Projects for Kids to Help the Elderly

Grade Level:	4–12
Skills Needed:	Writing
Time Required:	1 hour

46. Record a Memoir

You Can Help

It is said to be a fact, that the older you get, the clearer your earliest recollections can become. I'll have to admit that I believe that statement to be true. Often, I find it hard to shut those old memories out of my mind.

—*Thelma Bridges Sanderson Weymouth*

This great-grandmother had the foresight to record her childhood memories as a gift to her great-grandchildren. She is a capable writer at ninety years old and blessed with good health. Here is one of her stories:

My brothers still giggle when they recall one of their fondest memories of Grandpa. It happened on the Sunday of Grandpa's seventieth birthday. He and Grammy spent the day with us in Newfield. When the boys decided to walk down to the Little Ossippee River for a swim, Grandpa joined them. Having no bathing suit, and wanting to keep his underwear dry, he asked for a burlap bag and some string. In the two lower corners of the bag he cut leg holes. Once on, with the string, he hitched the top of the bag up over his shoulders. The boys were greatly amused to see their grandfather, dressed in a burlap bag, doing the breast stroke "just like a frog."

What a great gift to pass on to the children of future generations! Every senior citizen has stories like this one to tell. They are only waiting for someone to listen. Many seniors are not capable of writing their stories because of arthritis or weakness. Many of their stories will never be told.

Here's How

You can help an elderly person find renewed excitement for life and reinforce his or her self-worth by recording some memories about growing up.

1. Nursing homes are full of residents who would love the opportunity to tell someone about their lives. Even elderly people who have serious memory problems can often remember their youths in great and colorful detail.

2. You can visit an elderly person and write down the memories he or she shares with you.

3. After you record the stories, be sure to give the original and a few copies to the storyteller so he or she can mail them to family and friends.

Grade Level:	K–12
Skills Needed:	Varied
Time Required:	1–3 hours

47. Nursing Aides

You Can Help

For many elderly adults a nursing home will be their last home on earth. Some nursing homes let the patients decorate the rooms with their own furniture so that it feels warmer than a hospital room. Many nursing homes have pets that live with the residents, and they encourage patients to plant small gardens in the yard or in an attached greenhouse. All nursing homes plan special activities for the residents to keep them involved and busy with new things.

But nurses don't have the time to do the little things that separate one day from another for the elderly. The elderly have lots of time, and they like to do little things like spending an unhurried hour with someone reading a book aloud or playing a game of cards.

Here's How

The little things I suggest may not seem very important by themselves, but it is not the action, but the interaction that an elderly person craves.

Here are a few way for you to interact with the elderly patients of a nursing home or hospital:

- Deliver their mail and ask them if you can read it to them

- Fill up their water pitchers with fresh water

- Comb their hair

- Put lotion on their hands or feet (elderly feet get very sore)

- Read a book out loud to them (one chapter per visit)

- File and paint their nails

- Write letters for them

- Read the newspaper to them

- Record their memories in story form (see Project 46)

Grade Level:	K–12
Skills Needed:	Art
Time Required:	1–3 hours

48. Canned Hearts

You Can Help

For elderly residents in nursing homes, or elderly people that live alone in their own home, the days can be very long and lonely. Nights are often broken by sleeplessness and physical discomfort. The elderly who live in apartments or single family homes are especially isolated and may go for days without speaking to another human being. Even in nursing homes, elderly people may feel forgotten and left behind.

Many residents of nursing homes are suffering from memory deficit, and some people think they are too confused to be lonely. But we can't ignore their need for human interaction, or we will reduce them to animals. Recently a charming elderly woman explained to her family a difficulty that she was having. She would get a thought in her head, but she couldn't get it to come out of her mouth. It was very frustrating for her to think of an idea or memory she wanted to share, but to have the words locked inside her head. She was suffering from aphasia. Without her careful explanation, her family may have assumed that her verbal silence indicated a mental silence. Perhaps they would have made the mistake of treating her in a patronizing way. She had the wisdom to help her family understand her difficulty, but not all elderly people are able to explain themselves so clearly. When we work with the elderly, we should try to remember that silence is not a reflection of brainlessness, and that everyone deserves to be treated with dignity and respect.

Here's How

You can touch the lonely spirit of an elderly person with some simple artwork and an empty can.

1. Just decorate empty coffee or orange juice cans with colored paper. You can glue on artificial flowers, paintings, a poem, candy, colored rice, ribbons, or anything that you think an elderly person would like.

2. It is especially nice to personalize the cans by getting information about the elderly person from the nursing home and making the can just for her or him. When you call the nursing home, ask the nurse for the names (correct spelling too) and interests of some elderly patients. Then you can paint their names on the can and make designs that are special to them. Personalizing the cans tells the patients that you took the time to find out about them and that you cared enough to create something with only them in mind.

3. After you decorate the cans, you can fill them with different things. For the patient who likes gardening, you can fill the can with dirt and plant a little flower or some ivy (put some rocks in the bottom for drainage). For the patient who likes sweets, you can fill the can with his or her favorite candy (check with the nurse to be sure the patient can eat candy). For the patient who likes to write letters, you can fill the can with pencils and pens. For the patient who likes to play games, you can fill the can with playing cards and dice.

4. Use your imagination, but let whatever you put inside the can be a reflection of the dignity within the elderly person receiving it.

Grade Level:	4–12
Skills Needed:	Painting Cleaning
Time Required:	3–9 hours

49. Home Repairs

You Can Help

Many elderly people are desperately hanging on to their independence by living in homes that are dirty, dingy, and in some cases dangerous. They are physically unable to repair their own homes, and they can't afford to pay someone else to do the work. They may be afraid to admit that their homes are in ill repair, for fear of being declared incompetent and sent to a nursing home. One elderly woman fell while bringing in a bag of groceries with a friend. She begged her friend not to tell anyone, even though she was in terrible pain, because "if they find out I fell, they'll put me in a nursing home." Other elderly go without heat, straddle broken stairs, stuff sheets in broken windows, and live with dirt and mice just to preserve their independence as long as they can.

Here's How

You can help an independent elderly person repair, repaint, or clean his or her home. This is a wonderful team project. Several families can form a team to work on a home together, or a group of kids can form a team with a group of adults. Here are some of the things you can do to help an elderly homeowner:

- Rake the lawn and plant some flowers
- Trim the shrubs
- Scrape and paint a room, or two rooms
- Replace a carpet or shampoo a carpet

- Repair broken stairs and railings
- Mend cracks in walkways
- Plaster holes in the wallboards
- Fix broken shutters
- Replace broken glass
- Remove trash from the basement, attic, porch, or garage
- Wash floors and shake rugs
- Scrub the woodwork
- Replace lightbulbs
- Check on smoke detector batteries

Steps to Organize a Home Repair Team

1. Identify an elderly person or couple who need help with home repairs. A good source for names is the Visiting Nurse Association in your area (sometimes the local hospital will give out this number, or look under "Nurses" in the Yellow Pages). Also, social workers may be aware of elderly people who live alone in neglected circumstances.

2. Visit the home and talk to the elderly person about what needs to be done.

3. It is helpful to take someone with you who has a knowledge of home repairs, such as a contractor or builder.

4. Sit down with the elderly resident and the builder to make a list of what you would like to do and all the supplies you will need. Make sure the homeowner has liability insurance in case someone is hurt while working there.

5. Set a date to do the work. Try to limit the work to what can be done during one Saturday.

6. Put together a team of volunteers who can help with the repairs.

7. Ask local stores to donate the supplies you need. If you are going to paint any rooms, hardware stores may be willing to donate mismixed or outdated paints of the same basic color, but slightly different shades. Using a big pail, mix all the cans of paints together into one color before you start painting.

Grade Level:	K–12
Skills Needed:	Listening Calling
Time Required:	1 hour

50. Adopt a Granny

You Can Help

In generations past, children had constant access to the elderly in their community, and the elderly also had access to the children. It was a mutually beneficial relationship, with the young offering assistance with little chores, and the old offering comfort and wisdom. But intergenerational relationships are becoming rare. Families move around to follow jobs, and the generations have become separated and strange to one another. Many young children are actually frightened at the sight of elderly people. They have had so little experience with them that they see their wrinkles and bent fingers as bizarre.

Here's How

You can reconnect the generations and make an elderly person feel needed and involved again.

1. Adopt a granny or grandpa in your neighborhood or town. You probably already know of a lonely senior citizen

in your community, but if not, ask your pastor or Visiting Nurse Association to suggest someone.

2. You can treat your adopted granny or grandpa just like you would treat your real grandparents. Invite him or her to Sunday dinner, help with errands, exchange Christmas gifts, invite him or her to all of your family birthday parties, share your report card grades, ask advice about things, and listen, especially listen.

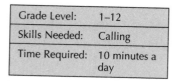

Grade Level:	1–12
Skills Needed:	Calling
Time Required:	10 minutes a day

51. Elder Call-In

You Can Help

Every morning, a third-grade class in Polk, Nebraska, calls several elderly residents to make sure they are well. Many elderly people live alone in houses or apartments where they may not see other people often. It is not uncommon for older persons to fall, break a hip or leg, and not be discovered for days. They could also lose their heat, their electricity, their phone service, run out of an important prescription medication, or just become too ill to answer the phone. Receiving a simple phone call each day from a caring young person is a great source of comfort to someone who lives alone.

Here's How

You can check on an elderly person each day by phone or in person. You can also ask your class or Kids Care Club to join the project and bring comfort to many elderly people each day.

1. You can get names of people to call from the Visiting Nurses Association or Social Welfare Department.

2. The first time you call the elderly person, tell him or her who you are and ask if you can call each day just to make sure he or she is feeling okay and has everything needed. Decide on a time of the day that is good for both of you. Try to be punctual about calling at the same time every day.

3. Most elderly people who live alone have a visiting nurse or a social worker who comes weekly. Try to find out the names and phone numbers of people you can call if the senior is sick or doesn't answer the phone one day.

Grade Level:	K–12
Skills Needed:	Cutting
Time Required:	1 hours

52. Clip Coupons

You Can Help

Older people like to save money. It doesn't matter if the savings go into their own pockets or to someone they care about. Perhaps it comes from living on a fixed income and knowing that pennies are worth something, or perhaps the years have developed their respect for a bargain.

When a basket full of clipped coupons was put on a table in a senior center, the coupons disappeared in minutes, even the ones for diapers! The seniors explained that they would like to give the diaper coupons to young families they knew (which made them feel as though they were contributing something). Since then, frequent baskets have gone the way of the first. Rumor has it that the seniors are using the best coupons as stakes in their bridge games.

Here's How

1. You can clip coupons from the newspaper or sales flyers and save them for elderly shoppers.

2. You can ask friends and neighbors to save coupons, too.

3. When you have saved a basketful, deliver them to a senior center close to you.

Note: Keep an eye on the coupon expiration dates. It is frustrating to try to redeem an expired coupon.

Grade Level:	K–12
Skills Needed:	Planting Watering
Time Required:	1–3 hours

53. *Nursing Home Blooms*

You Can Help

Residents of nursing homes are often in wheelchairs and walkers. For some, even the trip to the dining room can be exhausting. Taking a stroll through a pretty park in spring is no longer a realistic goal for them. The beauty of nature is limited to the plants in their room, pictures in magazines, and the view from their bedroom window. Some elderly like to sit for hours staring out their window because it is the only remaining contact they have with nature.

Here's How

You can enhance the view of nature for someone who can't get outside. You can plant flowers at a nursing home where residents can see them from their windows.

1. Ask a local plant store to donate the flowers or bulbs and any fertilizer they need to grow.

2. If the plant shop won't donate the flowers, you can have a fund-raiser and earn the money to buy them (see Chapter 10).

3. Ask the nursing home director for permission to plant the flowers, and she will direct you to a spot where the residents will be able to see them.

4. Be sure to return weekly to water and weed the flowers while they are growing.

5. Maybe you will make a few older friends while you are there.

Grade Level:	4–12
Skills Needed:	Writing
Time Required:	1–2 hours

54. Lend a Hand—Write Letters

You Can Help

My grandmother often felt guilty about not writing letters to her friends, relatives, and especially her grandchildren. Every few months she would try again, but her hand was too shaky and her wrist ached from arthritis. She would always decide to call on the phone instead. But long-distance calls were too expensive to make often, so her communication with family and friends was limited to birthdays and holidays. How she wished she could stay in touch with everyone she loved.

Many elderly people have trouble writing letters for the same reasons that my grandmother did. As a result, they feel out of contact with family members and old friends who have moved away.

Here's How

You can help an elderly person reestablish old relationships.

1. You can write letters for someone by writing down the words as they dictate them to you.

2. If it has been a while since the elderly person wrote letters, he or she may have some trouble getting started again. You can suggest things to write about, like a new address or phone number if the writer has recently moved, current events (political or family), church news, news about old friends in common, and seasonal observations on flowers, cold, humidity, etc. If the elderly person is writing to a child, he or she can ask questions about grades, sports, friends, favorite music, or television shows.

3. Encourage the writer to tell stories about his or her own past experiences.

4. Make sure to mail the letter for the elderly person, who may not be able to get to a mailbox easily.

Grade Level:	6–12
Skills Needed:	Mowing Raking Planting
Time Required:	2–6 hours

55. Killer Lawns—Landscaping

You Can Help

This was the first project of the Kids Care Club. Through a social worker in our town we heard about an elderly widow who was determined to live alone in her little house. She was quite weak and could not take care of her lawn. She hired a man to mow every few weeks, but she was living on a limited income and couldn't afford to have any raking, weeding, or shrub trimming done. Her home was almost obscured by shrubs which had run wild. Where once a charming flower bed had bloomed, there was now a mass of multispecied weeds. Old leaves were pushed in mounds under bushes and trees, and the patio, where she loved to sit during the summer, was covered with limbs and broken pottery.

Here's How

Fifteen teenagers from the Kids Care Club showed up one Saturday morning to help Mrs. Luckhurst with her lawn. They raked, weeded, mowed, trimmed the shrubs, picked up limbs and trash, and planted flowers around her patio and mailbox. They were finished in three hours, and Mrs. Luckhurst was beside herself with appreciation.

1. You can help an elderly homeowner maintain their yard and their health by volunteering to mow, rake, weed, and generally care for their yard.

2. Maybe you can team up with a group of friends, as the Kids Care Club did, or perhaps your family can do the lawn work together.

Grade Level:	10–12
Skills Needed:	Driving
Time Required:	1–4 hours

56. Chauffeur/Errand Runner

You Can Help

Grace gets around her apartment quite well. She has furniture or walls to hold for support while she walks from one room to another. Bending over is a little risky, sometimes ending in a fall. But Grace can no longer drive a car, so getting to doctor appointments and doing the weekly shopping are not always possible. She must wait for one of her sons to find the time to drive her. Even when her sons are able to drive her, she is dependent on special equipment to help her walk, and long grocery aisles are difficult for her to negotiate. Most of the time, for the sake of convenience, her sons do the errands for her. Grace is fortunate to have sons to care for her. Many elderly do not have anyone to help them with driving or errands.

Here's How

1. You can help an elderly person by driving him or her to doctor appointments, hair appointments, or to the bank.

2. You can also run small errands such as picking up medications, groceries, hardware, or other necessities.

3. This project can be expanded to provide a free delivery service for senior citizens through a local grocery store. Elderly people who are unable to drive could call the store with a grocery list, and the store could charge the food to their credit card. Then you would be contacted to deliver the groceries. Perhaps you could offer your free delivery service one or two afternoons each week.

4. You could advertise your service through posters in the store and by alerting the social workers, visiting nurses, and senior centers.

57–60 Kids Care Messages

You Can Help

The following four projects are ways to send messages of kindness and hope to elderly people in nursing homes. Each project is designed to be a one-time project, but can easily be expanded to be long-term. All four projects are great for groups of kids to do together. Although these projects will serve no practical purpose for the elderly recipients, they do bring the young and the old together and bridge the generations, and each project will make the elderly residents of a nursing home feel important and remembered.

Grade Level:	K–12
Skills Needed:	Coloring Art
Time Required:	2 hours

57. Care Cards

Here's How

You can make elderly patients happy by creating holiday cards for them.

1. A group of kids can get together and make heart-shaped cards for Valentine's Day, snowflake cards at Christmastime, four-leaf-clover cards on St. Patrick's Day, turkey cards at Thanksgiving, ten plague cards at Passover, and colorful egg-shaped cards at Easter.

2. Be creative and make the cards as wild and unique as you can imagine.

3. Deliver the cards to the nursing home and spend a little time with the patients there.

Grade Level:	K–12
Skills Needed:	Singing
Time Required:	2 hours

58. Carols of Kindness

Here's How

You can form a choir of kids that practice singing old hymns, Christmas carols, or oldies but goodies.

1. Get together a group of friends and rehearse the songs you would like to sing for an elderly audience.

2. It is fun for the elderly to be able to participate, so if you have access to a copy machine you can make lyric sheets to pass out and invite the audience to sing along with you.

3. This project requires that you make early arrangements with the nursing home. The nursing home director will have to schedule a room for your ''concert'' and post the invitation around the nursing home for a week or two before you sing.

Grade Level:	1–12
Skills Needed:	Coloring Writing
Time Required:	2 hours

59. Friendship Box

Here's How

This might sound like a silly project, but anyone who has spent time with the elderly will testify to how much they enjoy little things like this. One geriatric expert has stated that all elderly suffer from some degree of depression. This project is an anti-depressant cure which can be taken anytime, and as often as needed.

1. You can decorate a shoe box with cheerful construction paper or wallpaper scraps. Maybe you can write a short poem, a scripture, or a happy saying on the side of the box and decorate around it with ribbons, dried flowers, buttons, and funny faces.

2. In the top of the box, make a hole large enough for a hand to reach inside.

3. Fill the box with folded pieces of paper on which you have drawn happy faces or written funny jokes, beautiful poems, sweet sayings, or famous quotes (anything that would cheer an elderly person up).

4. The Friendship Box can be left at the nurses' station or in the dining room where patients can withdraw a happy thought whenever they need one. The nurse can also take the box on evening rounds to offer a little pick-me-up to patients who are bedridden.

5. You can find poems, jokes, quotes, and sayings in your library. Ask the librarian to help you. You can also ask the

elderly to contribute special poems or sayings that have made them happy over the years.

Grade Level:	K–12
Skills Needed:	Gluing Art
Time Required:	2 hours

60. Holiday Corsages

Here's How

You can turn a bunch of carnations and some safety pins into beautiful corsages and boutonnieres that will make a few elderly people feel beautiful for a holiday.

1. Just combine the flowers, lace doilies, ribbons, construction paper, and your imagination to make artful corsages and boutonnieres that will enliven the most tired of hearts.

2. Attach a large safety pin to the back so that the corsage or boutonniere can be pinned on a dress or jacket.

3. Deliver them to a nursing home on a special holiday.

Grade Level:	5–12
Skills Needed:	Hair dressing Personal care
Time Required:	1–2 hours

61. Beautician

You Can Help

All people feel better when they know they look their best. The elderly like to look nice too, but they may have lost the eyesight, flexibility, and strength to "pretty" themselves. Many elderly rely on nurse's aides or friends to help them wash, curl, and comb their hair, shave, and paint or file their nails. Some elderly get discouraged and give up trying to look their best.

Here's How

You can help an elderly lady feel pretty (inside and out) by combing, styling, or curling her hair, powdering her nose, applying her lipstick, painting her nails, and helping her put on her favorite jewelry. For an elderly gentleman, you can gel and comb his hair, help him use an electric shaver, splash on a little aftershave, and fix his favorite tie.

1. Many elderly women who live at home would love for someone to visit once a week to wash and set their hair in curlers. You may know someone in your neighborhood who would like some help with her hair each week.

2. You can learn how to do a professional job by watching beauticians in a salon before you get started.

3. Stick to washing and curling hair and don't be tempted to try cutting or coloring. If you made a mistake, the elderly lady would be upset (and not feel pretty), and you would feel badly, too.

4. Ask at your church, Visiting Nurse Association, or social welfare office for names of elderly people who would like this kind of help.

Grade Level:	K–12
Skills Needed:	Baking
Time Required:	2 hours

62. Birthday Care Cakes

You Can Help

It was the day of her eighty-ninth birthday. Hidden carefully inside the cold box was a carrot cake with frosting made from cream cheese and powdered sugar. On top of the cake were nine yellow candles, one for each decade of her life, and a blue written message which read Happy Birthday Mamie.

After dinner her son held the cake knee-high so that her great-grandson could light each of the candles. The family presented her with the cake in a crackling chorus of ''Happy Birthday.'' Mamie cried. In eighty-nine happy years she had never before had her own birthday cake!

We often think of birthday cakes as a child's birthday rite. But the elderly enjoy them, too.

Here's How

You can make this project as big or small as you like. You can decorate a cake for an elderly neighbor or relative once a year, or you can decorate birthday cakes for all the residents in a nursing home.

1. If a group of volunteers would like to bake cakes for a nursing home, one birthday party a month can be planned.

2. On the first of each month, you can bake cakes for all the residents with a birthday during that month.

3. You can present the cakes at a monthly birthday party to which all the residents in the nursing home are invited.

4. The birthday ''boys and girls'' can share their cake with all their friends, and everyone can celebrate together.

Note: Check with the nurse about what each birthday boy or girl can eat. Many elderly have food allergies or restricted diets.

Grade Level:	K–12
Skills Needed:	Sewing Drawing
Time Required:	1–6 hours

63. Lap Quilts

You Can Help

As people get older their blood circulation becomes slower, and so their feet, legs, and hands often feel cold. This condition is further aggravated for elderly people in wheelchairs because of their lack of exercise. Many elderly like to keep a blanket over their legs in the wheelchair to make up for the heat which their veins are not producing.

Here's How

You can make lap quilts for disabled elderly that will warm their legs and their hearts.

1. Using old sheets or inexpensive white cotton fabric, cut squares that are twelve inches by twelve inches.

2. With colored permanent markers or fabric paints, make cheerful designs on each square.

3. Sew the squares together, with the rough edges folded toward the back of the fabric. The quilt should be four or five squares wide, and six or eight squares long (long enough to cover the legs of someone in a wheelchair, but not so long so that it will get tangled in the wheels).

4. You can use a piece of warm flannel to make the back of the quilt. Sew it along all four sides and sew blanket binding to cover the rough edges.

5. This project is fun for a group of kids to do together, each decorating a square and sharing the sewing work.

6. It can also be expanded to make a large quilt with designs that reflect compassion and human kindness, which can be raffled off as a fund-raiser for some other project (see Care Quilt Raffle, Project 102).

Grade Level:	K–12
Skills Needed:	None
Time Required:	1–4 hours

64. Sandboxes for Icy Walkways

You Can Help

The children who live in snow-blown climates love winter with its promise of sledding, skiing, skating, and snowmobiling. But for the elderly the winter holds a much different promise. The elderly who live in cold winter climates are often isolated inside their homes by a realistic fear of falling on slippery sidewalks or steps. Many elderly are killed each year by staying out too long in frigid temperatures, shoveling heavy snow, or falling on slippery walkways. Sand is an effective tool for reducing falls on ice, but most elderly do not have easy access to sand.

Here's How

1. You can place containers of sand on the doorstep of elderly residents. They will be able to easily toss some sand on the steps any time they want to walk outside.

2. You can also place containers of sand on town or city walkways where elderly people are likely to travel.

3. Most communities will give you sand for this project at no cost. But if not, ask local merchants to donate to your sand fund.

4. Make sure to check the containers you place around town frequently and refill them as needed.

Grade Level:	10–12
Skills Needed:	Counseling
Time Required:	1–2 hours

65. *Senior Suicide Hopeline*

You Can Help

We often hear news reports about teen suicide and the devastating effect it has on the family and even on an entire community. Suicide hot lines and runaway hot lines have been established all over the world to help desperate young people find ways to deal constructively with their problems and not give up on life. We don't hear as much about the number of elderly suicides that occur every day around the world. But the fact is that elderly suicide is almost twice as common as teen suicide.[14]

Here's How

You can start a hot line for seniors who are lonely, scared, or just tired of being forgotten. You cannot solve their problems or relieve their pain, but a youthful voice may bring promise and hope back to their spirits. Sometimes all an elderly person needs is to talk to someone who wants to listen, someone who thinks he or she is important enough to "waste a little time" with. If the elderly person needs more than a warm voice on the other end of the phone, the call can be referred to counselors, doctors, or Alcoholics Anonymous if drinking is involved.

Some signs of potential suicide are:

- Giving away favorite things
- Verbal hints ("There's nothing to live for," or "Everyone would be better off without me.")
- Drug or alcohol abuse
- Changes in sleeping or eating habits
- Loss of interest in social activities
- Persistent sadness
- Loss of interest in appearance
- Romanticizing death ("Death is a warm and happy thing.")

1. This project requires more specialized training in crisis intervention and the issues of aging than the author is able to provide. Perhaps you can enlist a geriatric counselor, a psychiatrist, or a crisis intervention expert to provide you and other volunteers with training and ongoing support. You can get referrals for geriatric professionals from local nursing homes or retirement housing.

2. After you have an expert ready to train the hot line volunteers, you can recruit others to help answer the phone through your school or church. Perhaps some senior citizens will want to volunteer to help too. You can recruit seniors through posters at senior citizen centers, the YMCA, or retirement housing.

CHAPTER 8

Responding to Handicaps

When I was four years old, I was in a plane crash that paralyzed me and killed my father. I spent five months after that at Shepherd Spinal Center in Atlanta, Georgia. I liked it there very much. The nurses were very nice to me, although my memories are vague.

Every summer I go to Massachusetts. I have friends there and we do a lot of stuff. We love to go swimming and collect shells on the beach. As part of my therapy, I swam four to six hours a week for five years. That was fun because I got to know the instructor really well.

In the winter I go to Vail, Colorado, and go skiing. I've been skiing since I was in the first grade. I use a sit-ski that looks like a small kayak, and short poles to guide me. It is great fun, and because I am so low to the ground, it is harder for me to wipe out! There is also an instructor behind me holding on with a tether. Vail is really cool and I can get around without any assistance.

One thing that makes me a little uncomfortable is when little kids, or even kids my own age, stare at me. I know they don't know how to handle seeing someone in a wheelchair, but it makes me a little uneasy. Sometimes I just wave at them like I know them. Another thing that makes me uncomfortable is when people *try to help me when I can do it myself. They ask me if I need help when I'd prefer to do it myself. If I need help, I don't hesitate to ask anyone.*

My friends make me feel comfortable about being in a wheel-chair. They treat me as just another person. That's what I want to be seen as, just another teenager.

—Katherine Lowe, Georgia,
fifteen years old

Katherine Lowe visiting her great aunt. Behind: Katherine's brother, Chesley, and mother, Kathy.

Understanding Persons With Handicaps

Handicap: A disadvantage possessed by one person as compared with others.
> —New Lexicon Webster's Dictionary

A handicap is a disadvantage or a difficulty which affects some part of a person's life. There are many kinds of handicaps. Some affect a person's body and make it hard for him or her to walk or move, some affect a person's mind and make it hard for him or her to learn easily, some affect a person's senses and make it hard for him or her to see or hear as well as others, and some affect a person's environment and prevent children from growing up with the opportunities other children have. But all handicaps affect the emotions. All handicaps tend to make a person feel different from other people, separated and segregated. Sometimes people with handicaps feel as though they are less than human, defected, and not as important as "normal" people.

Perhaps a young boy has a reading handicap and doesn't learn to read until he is eleven years old. That would put him at a disadvantage with other children who learned to read at the age of five or six. He might even feel as though he is stupid when he compares his reading skills to the other kids his age. And, unfortunately, his teachers and his classmates might reinforce his poor self-image by showing impatience when he tries to read out loud, or teasing him about being lazy and not trying hard enough. But perhaps this same child is gifted at math or art or music. His handicap affects only one aspect of his life, it does not define him. In fact, Woodrow Wilson had the same handicap, and people called him "backward" and "slow" when he was a child. Thomas Edison couldn't write a readable sentence. Even Hans Christian Andersen had a handicap—he couldn't read! He told his beautiful stories to someone else who wrote them down for him. Many of the world's greatest contributors have been persons with handicaps.[15]

In this chapter we will not use the term "handicapped persons" but rather "persons with handicaps." It is a simple way of reminding us that the person comes first and the handicap is incidental to the person. Persons with handicaps should not be defined by their handicaps any more than a teenager should be defined by his pimples. Handicaps and pimples do not tell us anything about the real person inside. Katherine Lowe, speaking for all persons with handicaps,

> *Persons with handicaps should not be defined by their handicap anymore than a teenager should be defined by his pimples. Handicaps and pimples do not tell us anything about the real person inside.*

asks us to look beyond the limits of her handicap and look instead at all she *can* do, and at all she has to share with the world.

In order to better understand and help persons with handicaps, we need to know a little about some of the most common handicaps, and what causes them.

Physical Handicaps

A physical handicap is the inability to control one or more body parts. Some children are born with disorders that cause physical handicaps, like spina bifida, which is an opening in the spine that causes paralysis, or cerebral palsy, which interferes with the mind's ability to signal muscles. Other children and adults develop a disease called muscular dystrophy, which slowly destroys muscle tissue. And other children and adults are physically handicapped by accidents and injuries, like Katherine Lowe.

Sensory Handicaps

A sensory handicap is a weakened ability to use one of the five senses. The two most common senses to be affected are sight and hearing. Some people have sensory impairment from birth. It may have been caused by their mother's malnutrition while she was pregnant or by some disease she was exposed to. Sensory handicaps can also be caused by infection, fever, or certain types of illness while a child is growing up, or by accidents and injuries.

Speech Handicaps

Speech handicaps affect the ability of a person to communicate verbally with others. One of the most common speech handicaps is stuttering. Stuttering is not an indication that the mind works slowly, and it is not a reflection of intelligence. One of the most brilliant men I know has a stuttering handicap. But stuttering can be socially isolating and very frustrating for people with this handicap. Another speech handicap is aphasia, which is a failure to use oral language for communication. Aphasia is caused by brain damage which may be the result of an injury or a stroke. It can affect the way a person responds to questions or interacts in conversations.

Mental Retardation

Mental retardation means a slowing of the brain's capacity to process and retrieve information. It affects most aspects of a person's growth and development, from mental comprehension to physical coordination. Mental retardation can be caused before birth by prenatal malnutrition, infection, disease, or a genetic disorder. It can be caused after birth by head injuries, lead poisoning, poor medical care, disease, and malnutrition. There are various degrees of mental retardation, from mildly retarded to profoundly retarded.

Learning Handicaps

Learning handicaps or learning disabilities affect the brain's ability to process and retrieve information, but they are unlike mental retardation in that they affect only certain aspects of development. For example, a child might be extremely strong and athletic, and also very gifted in math, but that child might be hyperactive in class and unable to concentrate on studies long enough to learn the material. Hyperactivity, attention deficit disorder, dyslexia, hearing handicaps, and emotional disturbances are some causes of learning handicaps.

Environmental Handicaps

Environmental handicaps are caused by living in poverty situations with inadequate food, medical care, and opportunities for physical and mental stimulation. Children who grow up in poverty may get enough food to keep their bodies alive, but not enough to do their best work. When you skip a meal, your thoughts begin to get a little foggy, and concentration becomes harder as your hunger gets stronger. Many children go to school each day so hungry that they are unable to concentrate on their work. Their hunger puts them at a disadvantage with kids who had a full breakfast before they came to school. Hunger can also lead to a disorder called pica, which is a craving for unnatural substances. Hungry children with pica are prone to eat paint chips on the floor or the walls. In old homes and apartments, these paint chips often contain lead, which causes lead poisoning, brain damage, and possibly death. Children in poverty are also less likely to get adequate medical care when they are sick, and may have to "suffer through" illnesses longer than other children. Certain illnesses, when left untreated, can lead to permanent physical or mental damage.

Poor children do not have access to the same tools for learning that other children have; most do not have computers at home; many do not use the library; most have not been inside a museum or art gallery; few are given the opportunity to travel and see new places. This is called cultural deprivation and it is also an environmental handicap for poor children.

I hope, as you read about these handicaps, that you feel a

common bond with people who suffer from them. We are all handicapped in some way. Some handicaps are more obvious and difficult than others, but we all have weaknesses or limits that put us at a disadvantage with other people we know.

The injustice of handicaps is not the limit itself, but the reaction of society to the limit. For many children the emotional stress of being different, of not being accepted, is far more handicapping than the problem itself. Betty Osman, in her book *No One to Play With*, says, "Acceptance is the most difficult thing to achieve. Only when a child feels accepted with his differences can he begin to gain inner strength and the courage to persevere."[16]

Children with handicaps must fight for their self-esteem harder than other children do. Most young children grow up knowing they are pleasing to the adults around them. Every small accomplishment brings praise and renewed courage to try a harder task. For children with handicaps, things are different from the start. Many do not receive the happy praise and adoration of adults around them, but rather they sense the burden they cause for others. They may become fearful of trying new tasks, because failure is too painful and may mean added trouble for caregivers. While other young children are enjoying play dates and making trips to the zoo, these kids are enduring hospital stays and appointments for therapy. Often children with handicaps are not exposed to other children on a regular basis until they go to school. So they start school with more than one disadvantage; they are socially underdeveloped, they are afraid of failure, and they tend to isolate themselves. Unfortunately, their first experiences with other children may reinforce all their fears and further complicate their disadvantage. They may begin to feel stupid and incapable; they may become depressed, angry, withdrawn, unmotivated, disruptive, or even suicidal.

Most children with handicaps eventually learn to cope with their limits by developing their strengths. In many cases their

> *Most children with handicaps eventually learn to cope with their limits by developing their strengths.*

handicaps become a blessing. The handicap forces them to develop a drive to succeed. It teaches them how to fight harder than others. It inspires a desire to be a contributor to the world instead of a taker. Their handicaps give them a depth of insight, empathy, and compassion that most people don't develop.

Projects for Kids to Help Persons With Handicaps

Grade Level:	K–12
Skills Needed:	Smiling
Time Required:	None

66. Be Handicap Friendly

You Can Help

There is one thing that people with handicaps need and want more than quality medical care, more than handicap-accessible buildings and transportation. It is acceptance from you and me. They want to assimilate into ''normal'' social circles, to be one of the group, to be a contributing member of the community. They want to be recognized for their talents and their ideas, not for their limits.

Here's How

You can be handicap friendly by looking beyond the handicap to the person.

1. Just say ''Hi!'' when a person with a handicap passes by.

2. Don't assume that a handicap makes a person ''blind'' to people staring, or ''deaf'' to people whispering.

3. Don't participate in jokes about handicaps.

4. Treat people with handicaps like everyone else; don't baby or pity them.

Grade Level:	K–12
Skills Needed:	Walking Talking
Time Required:	1–4 hours

67. Give Sight to the Blind

You Can Help

For children and adults who are blind, the world is at their fingertips. Literally, the world as they conceive it can only be known through touching it. A person who is blind cannot look at a photograph and recognize faces in it; he must touch faces to recognize them, or hear a voice he knows. The beauty of a spring field alive with wildflowers, the excitement of a bird feeding her babies, the awe of a white-capped mountain range, and the thrill of new vegetables growing in a garden are gifts that our eyes give us. The person who is blind must run in the field and touch the wildflowers. He must hear the baby birds and feel the twigs in their nest. He must feel the vegetable plants growing a little more each day. When he touches and hears these things, he can see them in his mind's eye.

Here's How

You can help a person who is blind to see more things with his mind's eye.

    1. Contact an organization for the blind (see Appendix I) and get the name of a person who is blind and who would enjoy being your exploration buddy.

    2. Plan activities that give your buddy opportunities to feel and hear things that are new experiences for him or her. Maybe a field trip (to a field), or a nature walk, or a trip to the zoo, or a day at a farm, or a visit to a country fair, or an

evening at a concert, or swimming, or a party, or a pond, or a railroad station, or a city, or a camping trip.

3. Be sure to watch your buddy and keep him or her safe while you explore nature together.

Grade Level:	K–12
Skills Needed:	Cutting and gluing
Time Required:	2 hours

68. Texture Boards

You Can Help

For children who are blind, their fingers are their eyes. That means that their world is limited to what they can touch in their playpen or nursery. That is all they can see. They need more tactile (touching) experiences than other children because every new feeling creates a new image in their mind's eye.

Here's How

You can bring a child who is blind new tactile experiences on a texture board.

1. Sand and paint a piece of thin plywood. Round off any corners.

2. Collect two-inch squares of many different materials, like velvet, corduroy, wax, plastic grass mat, pebbles, yarn, cork, chalk, aluminum foil, dried fruit, bubble wrap, fake fur, sandpaper, seashells, sticks, etc.

3. Glue the materials on the board and label each one with fabric paint. (Fabric paint dries in a raised bead, so older

children and adults who are blind can feel the letters and read the word with their fingers.)

4. Donate the texture board to a nursery or hospital that helps children who are blind. Visit the nursery and watch the children enjoy your board.

Grade Level:	K–12
Skills Needed:	Puppy training
Time Required:	lots

69. Raise a Seeing Eye Dog

You Can Help

A Seeing Eye dog is specially trained to help people who are blind. The dog is able to lead people across streets, onto a train, up stairs, and around obstacles on the sidewalk. But more than a surrogate pair of eyes, the dog becomes a constant companion and friend for the person who is blind.

There are organizations that raise puppies to become Seeing Eye dogs. These organizations place puppies in foster homes with families who promise to love and train the puppy for one year and then give it away to a blind person. Many families participate in this program, but many more are needed.

Here's How

You and your family can bring home a puppy to love and care for.

1. Talk to organizations in your area about raising a Seeing Eye dog for them. (See Appendix I.)

2. You will be asked to housebreak the puppy and teach him simple commands. Specialized training is needed to teach the puppy how to lead people around obstacles and danger.

3. You will be asked to give the puppy to a person who is blind when he is grown and trained. Sometimes families become attached to their puppy and don't want to give him away. One little girl said, "I loved my puppy and I didn't want to give him away. But then I remembered that someone needed him more than I did, and I felt good because it was like we were working together to help someone."

Grade Level:	1–12
Skills Needed:	Reading Speaking
Time Required:	1–3 hours

70. Recordings for the Blind

You Can Help

Children who are blind cannot choose a book at the library to read. They are only able to read Braille. Braille is a system of raised dots that can be read by touch. Very young children, who have not yet learned to read Braille, must rely on others to read stories to them.

Here's How

You can read your favorite children's stories to a little boy or girl by tape recorder.

1. Contact an organization that serves people who are blind. Ask them if they know anyone who would like some

children's stories on tape. (Check Appendix I, or look under "Social Services" in the Yellow Pages of your phone book.)

2. Borrow or buy a good tape recorder and several blank cassette tapes.

3. Choose your favorite stories with descriptive words. (Some books rely on the pictures to tell much of the story. You must choose stories that use mostly words.)

4. Slowly and clearly, read the book into the tape recorder. Read only one story per side of the tape.

5. You can also use sound effects, like bells, horns, laughing, engines starting, or dishes falling.

6. Listen to the tape and be sure that it is easy to understand. You can remake the tape if you don't like the way it sounds.

Grade Level:	5–12
Skills Needed:	Drawing Measuring
Time Required:	1–3 hours

71. Raised Maps

You Can Help

Do you remember your first day in a new school? Were you a little nervous because you didn't know where the cafeteria was, or the bathroom, or the library? It probably didn't take you long to find your way around the school halls. But what if you were blind? Libraries, hospitals, and even schools post maps on the wall for us to see, but how can a person who is blind read the map?

Here's How

You can make raised maps that a person who is blind can read.

1. Start with a piece of stiff cardboard and glue a piece of smooth posterboard on top of it.

2. Choose a building to map. You can map your school, the town library, the theater, the grocery store, the university, a hospital, or any other place that a person who is blind would like to go. Ask permission to hang your texture map in the front hall or to leave it behind the desk where it is available to a person with impaired vision.

3. Measure the building you will map. How long are the halls? What size are the rooms? How far from one room to the next? You should make one map for each floor or department.

4. Draw a map on the posterboard using pencil. Try to keep the halls and rooms close to scale. (For example, if every foot of actual space was represented by an eighth of an inch on the map, then a sixteen-foot-by-sixteen foot room would be two inches by two inches on your map.)

5. When the lines on your map are correct, you can use fabric paint to trace the lines. Fabric paint comes in squeeze tubes, and you can trace the lines with the paint and leave a raised bead that can be read by fingers.

6. Also, using the fabric paint, label the bathrooms, elevators, stairs, cafeteria, and other important areas of the building.

Grade Level:	9–12
Skills Needed:	Sports
Time Required:	2–12 hours

72. Recreation Therapy

You Can Help

In Connecticut an organization named Pegasus helps kids with handicaps learn to ride horses. The Special Olympics organizes competitions to encourage kids to develop athletic skills. YMCAs offer swimming programs for kids with special needs. In Katherine Lowe's letter at the beginning of this chapter, she talked about skiing and what that sport has meant to her. Sports and recreation are fun and extremely important to kids with handicaps. It is a way to become like any other kid, a way to be accepted.

Here's How

You can help a kid with a handicap learn a new sport and reinforce his self-esteem too.

1. You can volunteer with an organization like Pegasus, Special Olympics, or the YMCA and work with the children they serve. (See Appendix I.)

2. You can volunteer to coach a sport at a school for children with handicaps.

3. You can just spend time with someone you know who has a handicap and teach him or her how to play a sport you are good at.

Grade Level:	1–12
Skills Needed:	Sewing Gluing
Time Required:	1–3 hours

73. Puppet Play

You Can Help

Children who have handicaps are often confused about social roles and rules. Sometimes they are frustrated and angry. Social skills must be learned just like math or reading skills. Dolls and puppets are tools to teach social skills and also a means of interacting with kids who are withdrawn and distrustful.

Here's How

You can make puppets to help kids with handicaps understand themselves and others.

1. You can use two pieces of felt, cut and sewn together around all the sides except the bottom, where the hand goes inside.

2. Use fabric paint or glue the felt pieces on the puppets to make them look like moms, dads, babies, girls, boys, teachers, doctors, nurses, police officers, firefighters, mail carriers, cooks, etc.

3. If you have enough materials, make puppets that have happy faces, sad faces, silly faces, lonely faces, scared faces, thinking faces, and naughty faces.

4. Donate the puppets to a school for children with handicaps and ask permission to visit the children and introduce your puppets.

Grade Level:	K–12
Skills Needed:	Memorizing
Time Required:	3–12 hours

74. *Learn Sign Language*

You Can Help

Children who are deaf or who have a speech handicap cannot speak the same language that other children can. They learn a special language called sign language. But unfortunately, the number of people these children can communicate with is limited to the number of people who know sign language.

Here's How

They can't learn your language, but you can learn their language. If every child learned to speak in sign language, people who are hearing or speech handicapped would not feel so left out of their world.

Following is the alphabet in sign language. You can begin to learn from this chart. Then ask your school, YMCA, church, or library to sponsor classes in sign language so that you and your friends can easily communicate with people who are hearing or speech handicapped.

A

B

C

D

E

F

G

H

I

K

L

M

N

O

P

Q

R

S

T

U

V

W

X

Y

Z

Grade Level:	K–12
Skills Needed:	Not seeing Not walking
Time Required:	1–3 hours

75. Walk a Mile in Their Shoes

You Can Help

How can you really know what it feels like to have a handicap? You can't. But you can experience a mimic-handicap for a little while and gain some insight into the complications of living within the limits it imposes. For example, try to get dressed some morning with a blind-fold over your eyes. Or try to grocery shop in a wheelchair. You will discover that some of the little tasks you can now accomplish without any effort are impossible with a handicap.

Here's How

You can increase your own understanding of a handicap and perhaps educate your community too.

1. Try the experiment mentioned above, dressing with a blindfold.

2. Ask your school to designate one day as Sight Awareness Day. Challenge all the students to come to school with one eye patched.

3. Contact a medical supply store or your Visiting Nurse Association about using a few wheelchairs for a day. Let different students take turns going to classes with the wheelchair. You might discover that your school is not very handicap friendly. Make a list of the difficulties you and your friends discover as you wheel through the halls, and present the list to your school board or principal.

4. Plan a wheelchair relay race in the gym during lunch break.

5. Take up a collection to buy a new wheelchair for a person who cannot afford to buy one.

Grade Level:	K–12
Skills Needed:	None
Time Required:	1–3 hours

76. Plan a Party

You Can Help

One of the greatest deficits for children with handicaps is the lack of opportunities to socialize with other children. Between the frequent hospital or doctor visits, private schools, and the special care they need, these kids become segregated from the rest of society. They are not often exposed to the same diversity in cultures and experiences that other children are exposed to.

Here's How

You can provide opportunities for children with handicaps to interact with other children.

1. Locate a school for children with handicaps or a group of children with handicaps that are interested in joining your ''Party Plan.''

2. The Party Plan invites several children with handicaps (up to ten kids) and several children from different cultural backgrounds and ages (up to fifteen kids) to participate in a monthly party.

3. The parties can rotate from one home to another.

4. The parties can be based on different themes or holidays, or they can include different charity projects, or you can make up group dances that incorporate wheelchairs, arms, legs, and singing.

Grade Level:	K–12
Skills Needed:	Nonspecific
Time Required:	1–3 hours

77. Comfort the Dying

You Can Help

Serious illnesses are handicaps, too. Cancer, AIDS, heart disease, and serious injuries keep people in bed and away from realizing their dreams. For many people with these and other illnesses, there is little hope of recovery. The doctors have done what they can, but the illness is too serious to cure.

Comforting the dying is a large part of Mother Teresa's mission in Calcutta. She tells many stories about those she has cleaned, fed, and cared for as they lived their final hours on earth. This is a difficult mission, not for the labor but for the tears. Mankind spends most of life avoiding death. But those who are dying have no choice in the matter; they must face death with courage and hope. We can support them in their painful last days with small acts of comfort.

Here's How

You can comfort a person who is dying and give his or her last days dignity and love.

1. Hospices are designed to care for people who are chronically ill and cannot be cared for at home. Many of their patients are dying. You can find a hospice in your area by calling the local hospital or looking in the Yellow Pages of your phone book. Also, AIDS facilities care for people who are fighting AIDS.

2. Call the hospice or AIDS facility and ask about visiting patients who are very ill and need extra comfort.

3. You can comfort the dying by visiting, reading to them, talking about things, singing to them, brushing their hair, pushing them in their wheelchair for walks, giving them sips of water, or doing whatever else they need.

4. Visit weekly if you can, and bring little gifts each time you come. (These can be cookies, a card, a newspaper clipping, a book to read, a jar of juice, a bag of raisins, candy, etc.)

5. There are some organizations that help critically ill children receive a last wish. You can volunteer to support their efforts. They are the Sunshine Foundation and the Make a Wish Foundation. (See Appendix I for addresses.)

Note: Parents, it is my experience that children are quite capable of accepting death when it is carefully explained to them and their questions are answered honestly. You might find some books in the library to help you talk to your children about death. Many funeral homes also have booklets which explain death to kids.

CHAPTER 9

Responding to Injustice

Justice

If you have a question about something you see
just be sure to not ask me
because I'm no authority.
I'm just an observer of this great game
and I wish that I knew who was to blame
for the hate and the fear and the pain
for the killers and con men, for the hopeless insane
for the thousands of generations that were born to die
for the millions of hungry and the never ending sky.
The hopeful and hopeless are one in the same
and there isn't anybody that we can blame
for the good and the bad that's inside me and you.
So until the great parade is finally through,
my friend, you know what to do
If you don't, don't ask me, I haven't a clue.

—Jason Heigl, fifteen years old

Understanding Injustice

Jason Heigl was the definition of justice. His story will help all of us understand justice through the eyes of a young idealist. When Jason was in eighth grade, he saw Sally crying in the lunchroom. Jason was new in school, but he had already made a lot of friends and was ''in'' most of the social groups at school. Sally wasn't in any of the groups. She had a learning disability and a speech problem that made her different from the others. Jason walked over to her and put his hand on her shoulder. ''Can I do anything to help?'' he asked. Sally looked at Jason. His eyes were deep brown, like a stained glass window that, despite the dark surface, couldn't dull the light behind them. She didn't know him, but somehow she trusted him. She gave him the letter that she held crumpled and wet in her shaky hand. Jason read silently for only a minute. It was a short letter, very to the point. It was a list of fifty kids in school who hated Sally. Jason's name had been put on the list, too. His expression changed and he rose from the chair beside her. ''This letter is not true!'' he said. Then he walked stiffly away, letter in hand, and slammed the lunchroom door behind him.

After school the girls who wrote the letter approached Sally. Her heart skipped several beats, and against her will, tears welled in her eyes.

''We want to apologize for the letter we wrote,'' said one of the girls. ''It was really mean and none of those kids hate you.''

Sally exhaled, then smiled and told them it was okay. She was perhaps too quick to forgive, but she was happy for the acceptance, even if it came from girls who had said such awful things only a few hours ago. As she waited for a ride home, she watched the girls walk down the path from the school. Then she saw Jason. He was waiting for them. She saw him talk with the girls. Then he moved aside and threw something in the trash. Was it the letter? She was sure it was.

By the next year, when Jason started high school, he was one of the most popular guys in school. He shared the good looks of his movie-star sister (Katherine Heigl), he was fun-loving, and he liked everyone. One morning, as he was passing through the halls of his high school, he overheard some kids calling a girl Fatso.

Her name was Linda. He watched Linda as she walked away, and he was furious. The next day he got to school early and waited for her. When he saw Linda arrive at school, he stopped her and asked if she minded if he walked with her to class. Jason went to school early every day after that to walk Linda to class. They became friends, and as Jason had wisely guessed, the kids didn't call her Fatso anymore. Linda was Jason's friend. Through his acceptance of her, the other students began to see her differently too.

Before anyone thinks of Jason as unique and too wonderful to emulate, he had his problems just as all teens do. His mother describes him as "her wild one" and suspected that he might have had a slight attention deficit. He had been known to skip classes and even to experiment with pot. His parents were beginning to worry about his performance in school. The high school in his town had an open-campus policy which treated the kids like college students. They could come and go as they wished, and class attendance was entirely their own responsibility. The policy seemed to work for some kids, but Jason, with all of his causes, was too quick to find "good excuses" not to go to class. His parents went to the school and asked his counselors and several of his teachers to be sure that Jason stayed in school for the entire school day. The school told his parents that Jason was responsible for the success of his own education and they would not baby-sit him.

On September 23 Jason climbed into a truck and left school with his friends. They were off for lunch at McDonald's. They never returned.

When his mother came home from shopping that day, the phone was ringing. It was the principal. The truck had been speeding to get back to school for the next class. The driver had lost control on a turn. Ironically, the accident had taken place just a few yards from Jason's home.

Jason's body lived for one week after the accident. A constant stream of his friends came in and out of his hospital room, and Jason's parents came to really know the child they had raised. They heard the stories about Sally and Linda, and many other eyewitness accounts of Jason's crusades for justice.

Jason died exactly one week before his sixteenth birthday. His parents made the difficult decision to donate his organs, because they knew Jason would have wanted one last chance to help others. Today, somewhere in Boston a young man lives and loves with Jason's heart, and somewhere in North Dakota a boy sees the world through Jason's eyes. Jason lives on.

This chapter is for you, Jason. A light so bright as yours cannot be destroyed, only splintered. Like a blazing coal that explodes into many small flames, you live on in the words you

Jason Heigl, facing camera, with his family and friends.

wrote, the souls you touched, the lives you saved, and the hope you still represent for all of us. This chapter is for all the things you would have done if injustice itself had not snatched you from us too soon.

Projects for Kids to Fight Injustice

Grade Level:	K–12
Skills Needed:	Empathy
Time Required:	None

78. *Pastel Discrimination*

You Can Help

When we hear the word ''discrimination'' most of us think of male versus female, Muslim versus Jew, or black versus white. If discrimination were colors, these would be bold, primary colors that are easy to see even at a distance. But most discrimination is more like a subtle pastel color which blends easily into its surroundings. Sometimes the contrast is so slight that even the victims don't recognize it.

Most everyone has been the victim of pastel discrimination. Discrimination happens every time someone is treated worse than others because he or she is different. Maybe you can remember times when the gang at school didn't like you because you were smart, or the kids made fun of you because you wore glasses, or the girls called you names because your clothes were hand-me-downs, or the boys ignored you because you didn't make the football team, and the list goes on. Jason Heigl was aware of the pastel discrimination against the girl with a speech impediment and the girl who was overweight. He was also known to walk away from anyone who made a racial comment or who classified people according to their hairstyle or clothes.

Here's How

This project will not define something for you to do, but rather it will suggest things for you to *not* do. Such as:

- Not participating in discussions that ridicule or make fun of someone because they are different

- Not being silent when someone is being hurt
- Not joining gangs or social groups that exclude people based on differences
- Not responding to discrimination with discrimination or violence
- Not laughing at jokes aimed at a particular race, sex, religion, size, or look
- Not judging others by what you see on the outside
- Not surrounding yourself with friends who look and think just like you
- Not letting someone sit alone at lunch because he or she acts "weird"
- Not being afraid to be friends with someone whom no one else likes
- Not trying to fit in with the popular kids by dressing and talking like them
- Not being afraid to be different yourself
- Not ignoring the differences in others (Notice and praise the things that make each person unique.)

Grade Level:	7–12
Skills Needed:	Writing Copying Stapling Interviewing
Time Required:	3–9 hours a month

79. Start an Outreach Magazine for Kids

You Can Help

Young people need an opportunity to voice their opinions about injustice, compassion, and human kindness in order for them to better define what they really believe. But where can young people be heard? The media does not represent the composite views of young people, and even teen magazines are written by adults who try to stay "in touch" with teen idols and fads. Society seems to have conspired to silence the generative minds of youth, yet they have so much to say!

A publication called *Border Crossing 1992* was created by high school students enrolled in an interdistrict course funded by the State of Connecticut and the New Canaan and Norwalk boards of education. The students conducted interviews with kids at ten area schools, urban and suburban. The thoughts of young people were compiled and expressed in words, photos, and art in the fifty-five-page booklet. Here is what some of the kids had to say:

I'm not scared; just don't shoot me or stab me. I want to die by myself.

Society influences everybody. There is not one person that's not influenced by society because you're either what is acceptable to society, or you are not.

The other day I was walking down the hallway with two

of my friends, who happen to be white, and one [black]
boy said, "Why are you hanging around with those
crackers?" and I was like "Crackers, I don't have any
crackers."

If I hurt someone, it's like a cycle, I hurt you, you hurt
me, it's endless.

Here's How

Like *Border Crossing*, you can give kids an opportunity to be
heard.

1. You can start an outreach magazine with two purposes. The first and primary purpose is to give young people
a forum for contemplating justice and peace. The second purpose is to offer kids ideas and inspirations for acting on their
principles.

2. Your magazine could cover topics like:

Child abuse

The death penalty

Hunger

Unequal education

Mercy killing

Racism (discrimination
based on race)

Ageism (discrimination
against elderly)

Handicapism
(discrimination against
persons with handicaps)

Abortion

Religious wars

Smoking

AIDS

Date rape

Homelessness

Ethnic cleansing

Anti-Semitism
(discrimination against
Jews)

Sexism (discrimination
based on sex)

Youthism (discrimination
against youth)

Violence

Sexual harassment

Terrorism

3. Teen writers and photographers could produce their

interpretations of these issues and their proposed responses to them.

4. It would be easier to publish a magazine with the help of your school, but even if your school won't help, publishing a magazine is not too difficult. All you need is access to a computer with a word processor to type your stories, a good printer to help you print a clean copy of your stories, a copy machine, and a camera with black and white film to provide photos for the magazine.

5. Print the articles horizontally on the paper, in columns.

6. Fold the papers in half, lengthwise, to create a magazine or newspaper effect.

7. On the front cover, under the name of your magazine, print the title of each article, the author, and the page numbers.

8. You can distribute the magazine through your school or church, or by leaving stacks in store windows.

9. Publishing a magazine can become expensive. You will have to pay for the copies, the film, the developing, and the transportation to do interviews. You can earn the money to pay the publishing costs by selling advertising in your magazine to merchants or services that target teenagers. You can print a copy of their business card in your magazine for a ten-dollar charge. You can increase your price as the magazine becomes successful.

10. Be sure to devote part of the magazine to projects kids can do to help others. If your magazine only defines the problem but doesn't offer solutions, it will be depressing to read. The readers and writers of a teen outreach magazine want chances to put their principles of kindness to work.

Note: If you are interested in creating a publication like *Border Crossing* at your school, you can write for more information to New Canaan High School, Attn: *Border Crossing* Director, Farm Road, New Canaan, CT 06840.

Grade Level:	5–12
Skills Needed:	Drawing
Time Required:	4–6 hours

80. *Community Services Map*

You Can Help

Most communities have more services available than residents know about. There are day-care centers for young children and the elderly, parks for walking and playing, skating rinks, swimming pools, nursing homes, hospitals, clinics, thrift shops, soup kitchens, rehabilitation programs, libraries, post offices, town halls, grocery stores, doctors' offices, dentists, social welfare departments, and churches.

Here's How

1. You can create a map of your community with only the major streets.

2. On the map, you can draw symbols or pictures for the different services in your town.

3. In the corner of the map, you can make a key that identifies each symbol or picture, the address, the service provided at that location, and the phone number.

4. If you make the map on legal-size white paper, it will be inexpensive to copy and distribute.

5. You can leave copies of your map with realtors, the Welcome Wagon (or any other service for new residents), visiting nurses, and social workers.

6. You can gather the information to put on your map by calling day-care centers, local schools, churches, recreation departments, senior centers, the Social Welfare Department, and by reviewing the Yellow Pages of your phone book.

Grade Level:	K–12
Skills Needed:	Talking Listening
Time Required:	1–2 hours

81. Kid/Parent/Teacher Association

You Can Help

I was recently asked to participate on a committee to solve a very controversial issue in our town. The issue involved a conflict between parental rights and teen freedoms. The assistant principal of our high school, Gary Fields, wisely recruited kids from each grade to sit on the committee, too. Some of the adults were opposed to kids on the committee because they felt that the kids were too young to understand the complexities of the issue and too emotionally involved to be objective about a solution. The first two meetings seemed to prove their fears, as committee members took sides and threw opinions at each other like javelins. But after the kids were certain that we had heard their feelings loudly and clearly, they began to focus on the solution. While the adults on the committee continued to feud, the kids got busy developing a compromise. They presented their plan, supported it with practical ideas, and eventually convinced all of us that it would work. The plan was passed unanimously.

Kids have solutions to many of the problems that adults struggle with. If adults take the time to explain the issues, void of condescension or intimidation, the kids can be helpful and supportive in the solutions. And when kids are part of the problem-solving process, they take ownership in the solution and work toward its success.

Here's How

You can organize a kid/parent/teacher organization in your school that gives kids a voice in the decisions that affect their school.

1. Talk to your principal, parents, or PTA about giving kids the opportunity to participate in making decisions about your school.

2. If the school is not receptive, you can write to your school board or to the editor of your local or school paper. Don't give up. Parents and teachers want the best for you, and eventually they will give you some say about what that is.

Grade Level:	3–12
Skills Needed:	Clipping Writing
Time Required:	2–4 hours

82. Positive Press

You Can Help

There is no shortage of bad news in our world today. Newspapers and television are full of the gory accounts of riots, murders, famine, and natural disasters. Bad news is the best news for selling papers and TV advertising.

It is easy to lose your perspective on the world and begin to see everything through lenses splattered with blood and suffering. Such negative vision robs people of hope and courage. After years of this assault on the human spirit, we may give up on compassion and kindness and decide that the world is too far gone to be worth any real effort. But the world is not all bad. For every bad thing that happens, there are many good things happening at the same time. We don't hear much about the good things because bad news sells more papers. But somewhere right now a baby is being born. Somewhere a girl is going on her first date. Somewhere an old widow is falling in love with an old widower. Somewhere a homeless man got a job. Somewhere a teen helped his neighbor. Somewhere a poem is being written. Somewhere a life is being saved. These are reasons to believe in human kindness. We need to hear more good news so that the good each person does will grow bigger and overshadow the violence and hate.

Here's How

You can do many things to bring attention to the good in the world.

1. You can clip articles from newspapers and magazines that tell stories about compassion, miracles, or achievements by kids.

2. Copy the articles and share them with your friends, teachers, and church leaders, or ask for a bulletin board or wall in your school on which to tape articles as you find them.

3. If you like to write, you can search out your own stories of kind and remarkable news. You can write the stories and have them published in your school paper or local paper.

4. Maybe the newspaper will allow you to write a weekly column about kids doing good deeds.

5. I would love to hear about the compassionate things that kids in your town are doing for others. You can send your stories to me at:

> Deborah Spaide
> c/o Carol Publishing
> 600 Madison Avenue
> New York, NY 10022

Be sure to include your name, address, and phone number in case I want to use your story in another book about kids caring.

Grade Level:	6–12
Skills Needed:	Movie viewing Writing
Time Required:	3–4 hours

83. Be a Movie Critic

You Can Help

Most large newspapers have a movie critic on staff who is paid to view the popular movies and write a report about them. If you have ever read a critic's report and then watched the movie, you may have wondered if he saw the same movie you did. Critics view movies through their own experiences, age, mood, education, and interests. Unfortunately, adult critics cannot analyze a movie from the perspective of youth, although young people are a major target for the movie industry. Shouldn't someone write about movies with a young person's view in mind?

Here's How

You can become a teen movie critic.

1. You can watch movies when they are first released and write a report for your local or school newspaper.

2. Avoid giving away the whole story, but give enough information to help the reader decide if he or she wants to see the movie.

3. You can report on the amounts of violence, bad language, sex, and discrimination against racial groups, women, the elderly, and so on. Does the movie have a moral? Is the message behind the movie one of peace and hopefulness, or violence and brutality? Some kids may have developed a taste for violence, and in their case your report will go unheeded. But other teens are sick of it and will appreciate your warning before they spend their money on a ticket.

Grade Level:	K–12
Skills Needed:	Shouting
Time Required:	none

84. The Code of Silence

You Can Help

Crime is a form of terrorism. It assaults and dehumanizes the spirit of society, forcing even good people into a conspired silence of survival.

The code of silence is our present-day serpent in Eden, appearing as a virtue, laden with empty promises, and ending in death. Honesty, courage, and compassion are virtues. Silence in the face of crime is not a virtue; it is cowardice.

Jeremy was eighteen. His life in the city made him feel fifty. He knew his way around the streets and the people. Jeremy worked nights at a small bar one block from his home. One night as he waited tables, he overheard some men whispering about a "hit." Jeremy didn't mean to overhear them, but as luck would have it, he just happened to be close when they were discussing some important details, like the time and place of the hit. It would take place the next night at the victim's home. Jeremy knew these men and they knew Jeremy. They trusted him to keep their secrets—the code of silence. Jeremy had to admit that he was a little flattered at their confidence in him. But that changed in a moment of horror when Jeremy realized that the hit was his best friend's dad. What would he do? The code of silence demanded he do nothing, pretend he had not heard a thing. But love for his friend demanded that he warn him. Even if he warned his friend and averted the next day's fate, the hit would be carried out by someone else, on another day. The only real protection was to call the police and hope they could find out who wanted his friend's dad killed. But talking to the police would make him a "snitch"—a breaker of the code. What would you do?

The conflict for Jeremy was one of values. He believed that the code of silence was a value he could live by, but when it opposed his value of love for family and friends, he was confused and scared. Many people suffer from this same allegiance to a false virtue. Some have even died to protect it.

Here's How

You can take a stand against crime by refusing to honor the code of silence. You can do this on a personal level, or you can start a movement with others.

1. You can talk to your class, Kids Care Club, scout troop, youth group, or Sunday school about the code of silence, and ask them to help you design a campaign to "Break the Code."

2. You can make posters that encourage people to stand up and shout against crime and put the posters around town in stores, on streets, and in school halls.

3. You can go into classrooms and teach younger kids how and when to speak out against crime.

4. You can organize "shout-outs" for drug-infested

neighborhoods, crime-ridden schools, or up and down the streets of your town. Invite people to gather and march while shouting anticrime slogans and carrying anticrime signs.

5. You can start a peer support group or hot line for people who need some extra courage to shout against crime.

Grade Level:	7–12
Skills Needed:	Reporting Interviewing Videoing Editing
Time Required:	4–8 hours

85. Make Social Awareness Videos

You Can Help

In this day of video cameras and VCRs, anyone can become a movie producer or talk show host. Amateur videographers have documented earthquakes, tornadoes, racial beatings, births, deaths, and many other pictures of real life. A carefully created video can tell a story, promote a cause, teach a lesson, give a workout, or sell a commodity. Why shouldn't videos teach people to understand each other and practice kindness?

Here's How

You can create a video that gives the youthful perspective on social issues like discrimination, crime, war, violence, and poverty. You can work alone or with a group.

1. Begin with researching the issue and writing a report which you can read to the camera while filming something that is relevant to your cause. For example, if you were mak-

ing a video on child abuse, you could read the definitions and statistics about abuse while filming children on a playground.

2. Try to include interviews with experts and victims on your tape, as well as interviews with young people who have opinions or ideas about the issue.

3. The finished tape can be offered to classes that are interested, church groups, and local cable television stations, or left in the library at school for kids to take home overnight. (For ideas on topics for tapes, see Project 79.)

Grade Level:	5–12
Skills Needed:	Writing
Time Required:	1–2 hours

86. Write to Lawmakers

You Can Help

Human rights are dictated by the principle of justice. The principle of justice is an offspring of the principle of love. If love ruled our world, we'd have no need for laws or courts or prisons, because no one would intentionally violate another. But love doesn't rule our world, and the rights of the weak are buried each day in hunger and violence and greed.

Most of us know when a human right has been violated. We know it on a level that rises above logic and law. When the black people in America were enslaved by rich white people, many people knew that human rights were being abused, but there was no law to prove it. When women were not allowed to vote, many people, male and female, knew that a human right was at stake, but they had no legal recourse to change it. And today children who live in the inner city are not getting the same education or opportunities to grow as children who live in suburbia, but there is no law to protect them.

Much of this chapter is devoted to helping young people find ways to be heard. Youth has a vested interest in the decisions made by the world on their behalf. Kids have the right to understand the issues and form opinions about them. They have the right to participate in the lawmaking process and have some degree of influence over their own future.

Here's How

You can influence the laws that govern your world by simply writing a letter. One example of the power of one kid with a pen is the story of eleven-year-old Samantha Smith. Samantha had heard all the fearful stories about nuclear war and atomic bombs. Many Americans were afraid the Russians would send a nuclear bomb to America and kill everyone. So Samantha Smith sat down and wrote a letter to then Soviet President Yuri Andropov, asking him to put away his bombs. Andropov was so touched by her letter that he wrote back to Samantha and invited her to visit his country. Samantha accepted his offer and traveled to Russia with her family and many American reporters. Through Samantha's eyes, America saw the Russian people as farmers, workers, fathers, and sisters. Samantha's letter changed the way a whole country felt about another country.

Your letter may not result in an invitation to visit a foreign country, but it might help some government official begin to see the issue through your eyes. Your letter might make a big difference.

1. If you and your friends would like to do this project together, you can start a letter-writing campaign and barrage the lawmakers with letters.

2. You can also write one letter and get everyone to sign it, although this doesn't have the same impact as a lot of individual letters.

3. You can get the names and addresses of lawmakers from the phone book, political headquarters, or voter registration offices.

Grade Level:	5–12
Skills Needed:	Advertising Organizing
Time Required:	4–40 hours

87. Our Community Cares Day

You Can Help

When the earthquake of 1990 tumbled homes and roads in California, people came from all over the United States to help. They came from every race, social group, and economic status to work side by side to rescue and relieve the victims of disaster.

Hurricane Andrew in Florida created a similar instant community of volunteers and goodwill as corporate presidents worked beside teenage gang members to feed and house those hurt by the devastating power of nature. And all of us were touched by the selflessness of Midwesterners as they worked together against the force of two floods during the summer of 1993.

Isn't it interesting that humans seem to be able to put aside their differences, prejudices, and greed when the cause is severe and *they are needed*. What a shame that we see this kind of community effort only when disaster strikes.

Here's How

You can initiate Our Community Cares Day, a day of human kindness.

1. Begin by picking a day and advertising it through posters around town, flyers sent home in school, radio public serv-

ice announcements (these are free), and an article in your local paper.

2. Groups of people can plan charity projects for the special day. Some people can volunteer to work in a soup kitchen or nursing home or visit sick children in the hospital. Others can volunteer to repair an elderly widow's front porch. Small children can give flowers or cards to lonely neighbors.

3. Everyone can be encouraged to perform an act of kindness for anyone they happen upon that day.

4. The goal of the day is to get people who don't normally volunteer to hear their own voice of charity and put it into action. We hope they will enjoy helping others enough to make a habit of it.

5. If you are working on this project with a group of kids, you can also plan activities for that day. You can schedule a march or parade, a Kids Care project, a bike race, a circus, a dance, a sports event, an awards ceremony, or a family picnic for everyone who volunteered.

Grade Level:	K–12
Skills Needed:	Drawing
Time Required:	1–2 hours

88. Justice Wall Mural

You Can Help

A picture is worth a thousand words. Artists have used paint and chalk to say many wonderful things. They have reminded us of nature's beauty through landscape paintings. They have made us cringe at brutal deaths and slavery. They have called us to celebrate new life and love and courage without a word being spoken. Pictures are more powerful than words because they send a message straight to our heart, unlike words, which must be mentally translated into images. Artists can freeze a time and place and put it before us so that we don't forget the lessons we learned and the ideals we formed.

Here's How

You can send messages of justice, courage, and compassion to your community by creating a Justice Wall Mural. This project is great for a family, a group of kids, or even a whole school to do together.

1. Every kid can make a picture that reflects justice or kindness or some other virtue.

2. The pictures can be made on individual sheets of paper and taped together on a hall or classroom wall, or each kid can draw his or her picture on a wall-size piece of mural paper.

3. Remind all participants to sign their names to their art.

4. Perhaps your school will agree to give awards for the three best illustrations of justice.

5. Invite the local newspaper to photograph the mural and interview some of the artists for an article.

Grade Level:	K–12
Skills Needed:	Watching Phoning
Time Required:	None

89. Neighborhood Crime Watch

You Can Help

Neighborhood Crime Watch is a group which organizes residents on a street or in an apartment building to keep an eye on their neighbor's property. They are told what to watch for, and they report any suspicious activity to police. The concept has been very successful, and many communities have a Neighborhood Crime Watch group at work.

Neighborhood Crime Watch is a new name for an ancient concept. In the past, and even now in many places, neighbor instinctively helps neighbor. But today people move so fast that many don't know the names of their neighbors. Kids, because of the school community, have a better chance to get to know their neighbors than adults do. So why shouldn't kids become players in the Crime Watch community?

Here's How

1. You can start a Neighborhood Crime Watch on your street or in your apartment complex.

2. Ask other kids in your neighborhood to join, too.

3. The local police will talk to you about what to watch for and what to do when you see something suspicious.

4. Perhaps your neighborhood already has a Neighborhood Crime Watch group. Ask them to let you and your friends join.

Note: Remember that your job is only to *watch* and report suspicious things, not to investigate them. No matter how tough you are, you are not a fair match for a bullet. Let the police do the investigating.

CHAPTER 10

Fund-Raising Activities for Kids

The hard fact is that most charity projects require a little cash to make them work. This chapter is intended to offer fund-raising ideas to support the previous charity projects. Most fund-raising projects are not great developers of the spirit of charity, unless they are a means to the end.

It is good for kids to be involved in the full cycle of each charity project. They should help with developing the idea, making the plans, organizing the tasks, raising the necessary funds, shopping for the supplies, and executing the plan. The kids will have more ownership in the results if they earn the money themselves instead of asking parents to pay for their kindness.

A covert benefit of fund-raisers is that they also raise awareness of the issue. For example: Perhaps a Kids Care Club decides to have a car wash to earn enough money to buy Christmas gifts for children with AIDS. They choose a location on a busy street and appoint two kids to hold signs by the road for drivers riding by to read. The signs say

CAR WASH
$5.00
HELP KIDS WITH AIDS

Many people passing by the car wash will read the signs. Some will stop, but even those who don't stop may start thinking about kids with AIDS and do something else to help them.

Following are a few fund-raising activities that will help you earn the money you need to do something wonderful for someone who needs you.

Fund-Raising Projects for Kids

Grade Level:	K–12
You Will Need:	Buckets, car soap, garden hose, sponges or rags, towels, cash box, change, signs
Time Required:	6–8 hours

90. Car Wash

This is a popular project for kids to do together.

1. The hardest part of this project is finding a good location for the car wash. You will need to be close enough to a busy street to get customers, have enough room off the street to wash the cars safely, and have access to an outdoor water faucet.

2. Once you have found a location and a date for your car wash, you will need to make signs and gather the equipment you will need. Don't forget the cash box (or shoe box) and enough one-, five-, and ten-dollar bills to make change for your customers.

3. It is fun to make an assembly line, with a few kids holding signs by the street to attract customers, a couple of kids taking the money, some kids washing the cars, some rinsing the cars, and some drying the windows with rags and saying "Thank you!"

4. Ask parents and teachers to help you determine a fair price for your car wash. You need to get enough per car to pay for your supplies and make a profit, but you can't charge too much or you won't get any customers.

Grade Level:	K–12
You Will Need:	Boxes or bags, flyers, transportation
Time Required:	3–6 hours

91. Recyclables

I remember as a child walking with friends in search of empty bottles. We would always find a few in the ditch along the road's edge. We would happily take our bottles to the country store at the corner, dirt and all, and use the refunds to buy ice cream.

1. You can collect bottles, cans, and other materials, in some states, for refunds and use the money to help others (instead of buying ice cream as I did).

2. You can write a letter to all the kids in your school, church, or neighborhood, asking them to collect recyclables to help needy people. If you have a charity project in mind that the recycled materials will finance, you can tell everyone about it in the letter. They may be more willing to help if they know exactly what the money will be used for. Be sure your letter lists the recyclables you want to collect, or else you will end up with a lot of things you don't want. Also, give an address for dropping off recyclables or a phone number people can call for more information.

3. Before you decide what materials to collect for recycling, find out what your state recycles and where you must go to redeem the material. Soda bottles are easily redeemed at most grocery stores, but other materials may be harder to redeem. Look in the phone book under ''Recycling Centers'' or ''Redemption Centers.''

Grade Level:	2–12
You Will Need:	Ice cream or ice cream maker, scoop, cones, cooler, ice, napkins, cash box, change, table, plastic tablecloth, signs, bell, sprinkles optional
Time Required:	3–5 hours

92. Ice Cream Stands

This project is a first cousin to the lemonade stands along the streets in the summer. Kids set up a table with goodies to sell to passersby. Lemonade is tempting on a toasty day, but ice cream is tempting anytime.

1. In choosing a spot for your ice cream stand, keep in mind that people are less likely to stop if they are driving than if they are walking by you.

2. Maybe you could get permission to set up your ice cream stand at a ball game, a beach, the local park, in a shopping plaza, on the street a parade is going down, or on the front lawn of your church after services.

3. Fill a large cooler with ice and arrange one, two, or three half gallons of ice cream with ice surrounding them.

4. Your ice cream cones should not be too expensive, or customers will go to an ice cream parlor with twenty flavor choices instead of only three. Make your ice cream a delicious bargain.

5. You could also make homemade ice cream if you have

a churn. Making ice cream is fun, and customers are even more tempted by homemade ice cream than the store-bought kind.

Grade Level:	5–12
You Will Need:	Herb teas, hot water, tea pots, tea cups, spoons, sugar cubes, milk, napkins, cookies, tables, tablecloths, chairs, centerpieces, other activities optional
Time Required:	3–8 hours

93. Children's Tea Party

You can have a benefit tea party at your school, church, library, community center, city pool, nature center, zoo, or in your own neighborhood.

1. Make invitations out of plain paper folded like a napkin. Ask people to purchase "tea tickets" for themselves, their children, and friends of their children. Send invitations to all the students in your school, hand them out in your neighborhood, place stacks in the grocery store, and tape one on the community bulletin board at the library or YMCA.

2. Offer a phone number on the invitation for parents to make reservations. Your customers can pay when they get to the party.

3. Set up each table with a tablecloth, a centerpiece, spoons and napkins and teacups for each place, a creamer and sugar bowl, and a plate of cookies.

4. You can make the tea ahead of time and keep it in large insulated containers. Pour it into pretty teapots to serve it to your customers.

5. You can also plan entertainment for the children, such

as games or a charity project that is simple enough for everyone to participate in.

Grade Level:	6–12
You Will Need:	Clothes Microphone
Time Required:	6–12 hours

94. Fashion Show

I've been to fashion shows with very young, and often unwilling, child models. The parents loved to watch the toddlers wander down the aisle dressed in fancy new clothes. But this project could be very successful for teens too, especially if the fashion show had a theme like wild wear, or swimwear, or jungle garb, or yesterday returns, or no-name wardrobes.

1. You can have a fashion show in your school or community center. Ask permission to use the auditorium, cafeteria, or gym, and set a date.

2. You will want to ask some local clothing stores to let you borrow a few outfits for the show. They would get free advertising and perhaps a few sales, too. Talk to them about donating a percentage of any sales generated by your fashion show to the charity you want to benefit.

3. You will also need a number of models. When asking kids to model, try to select a few of various shapes and sizes, not only tall and thin. Also, include boys and girls in your modeling group.

4. Advertise your fashion show with many posters all over school and town. Put flyers on windshield wipers, and ask your local paper to write a feature article about the show and the charity project it will benefit.

5. Assign several kids to be at the doors early to collect the viewing contribution as people come to your fashion show.

6. Someone will have to be the official master of ceremonies and announce the models as they come on stage (or down the hall or through the door) and also tell where each outfit comes from and how much it costs.

7. You can also create a written program to hand out at the door which explains your charity project, lists all the models, and thanks all the shops that provided clothing for the show.

8. As an added attraction, you can persuade some teachers or even the principal to model some funny outfits.

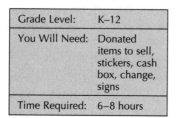

Grade Level:	K–12
You Will Need:	Donated items to sell, stickers, cash box, change, signs
Time Required:	6–8 hours

95. Yard Sale/Auction

Yard sales are a serious attraction in many parts of the world. People love a bargain, and many bargains have been discovered at yard sales.

1. You can ask your Kids Care Club, class, church, or school to collect used furniture, decorations, clothing, and appliances for a yard sale.

2. You can hold the yard sale at your school, a local business, a church lawn, or in your own yard.

3. Newspaper classified ads are a great way to advertise your yard sale. Be sure to mention that the sale will benefit a charity and has contributions from many donors.

4. Put signs on corners around town which direct people to the location and give the date of the sale.

5. Set up the yard sale with attention to displaying as many items as possible. Price each item with small stickers. Make sure the price you ask is a bargain and prepare to take offers for less.

6. Expect people to show up on the day of your sale one or more hours before it begins.

7. You can hold an auction with a few of the more expensive and desirable items. Choose a master of ceremonies to take bids and decide the sale.

8. After the sale, be sure to take down all the signs you put on corners around town.

Grade Level:	K–12
You Will Need:	Artwork, price tags, cash box, signs, flyers
Time Required:	1–8 hours

96. Art Sale

You and your friends can hold an art sale to benefit a charity project. You can sell paintings, pencil sketches, collages, sculptures, or photographic art which you or any young person has made.

1. Ask your friends and the art teachers in your town to encourage kids to contribute works of art to your art sale for charity. The only requirement is that the art reflect humans caring about each other.

2. Display the art in the local library or in your school lobby prior to the sale.

3. You can make copies of a piece of art to use as flyers or invitations to advertise the sale.

4. The sale can take place at a specific time, or it can be silent bidding. Silent bidding is easier because it allows people to shop at their leisure. If you use silent bidding, place a box close to the art display with a pad of paper. On a poster above the box explain how the bidding system works. You might explain it like this:

Charity Art Sale

Silent Bidding Rules:
On a piece of paper write your name, the name of the art you would like to purchase, your phone number, and the price you would like to pay. Drop your bid in the box. We will contact you by [give date].

Grade Level:	5–12
You Will Need:	Food from different cultures, tables, tablecloths, costumes, flatware, paper plates, cups, coffee, cream, sugar, napkins, centerpieces, signs
Time Required:	6–20 hours

97. Around-the-World Dinner

This project is a great way to make money and to celebrate different cultures in your community. It can even be educational.

1. To prepare for this project, you and your friends should find out where your families originated from. Most families have a history of migration from one country or culture to another. Find out what foods were common to each origin country and if the people of that culture wore any unusual clothing.

2. Get together with your friends and compile a list of the different countries you came from, the foods people eat in those countries, and the clothes they wear. From this list you can create a ''world-class'' menu! Choose interesting dishes from each country and put them together to make a balanced meal. Decide on a price for your meal. Assign each of your friends one part of the dinner to cook or buy.

3. Ask your school to let you use the school cafeteria for the dinner and the school kitchen for warming foods only. You should cook the dishes at home and bring them already prepared to the school.

4. Put posters around the school and hand out flyers inviting kids to come and bring their parents. Also, ask teachers if you can speak to their classes about coming to the dinner.

5. Sell tickets so that you will know how many guests to prepare for.

6. On the night of the dinner, cover the tables with tablecloths and arrange a centerpiece on each one. You can seat people at tables and bring them plates of food, or you can serve the food buffet-style. (You could still serve beverages at the table.)

7. Ask your friends to wear costumes that reflect their origin country as they serve tables and help with the dinner.

8. Try to persuade some parents or grandparents to perform little songs, dances, or stories from their origin countries after dinner.

Grade Level:	K–12
You Will Need:	Pledge sheets
Time Required:	2–8 hours

98. Marathons

Kids love marathons because they test their endurance and strength. There are as many ideas for marathons as there are activities in the world. The more creative your marathon is, the more attention it will get.

1. You can plan one of these marathons, or make up one of your own:

Chess	Spelling
Hopping	Skating
Dancing	Bowling
Swimming	Eating
Sewing	Corn shucking
Walking	Bike riding
Stroller pushing	Card playing

2. Find a location for your marathon and set a date.

3. Advertise your marathon through the schools, the YMCA, the churches, the scouts, the newspaper, cable TV, and flyers.

4. Get people to sign up for the marathon and give them two pledge sheets with carbon paper in the middle. Make sure the pledge sheets identify the charity project you are hoping to finance with the profits from the marathon. Sponsors will be more generous if they know they are helping the needy.

5. Collect one of the pledge sheets at the marathon. Ask the participants to collect money from their sponsors and mail it to you before a specific date. You should have copies of the pledge sheets, so you will know who has collected and who has not collected their pledges. You may have to call to remind late collectors.

Grade Level:	7–12
You Will Need:	Posters, flyers, change, prizes, games, activities
Time Required:	10–40 hours

99. Picnic Fair

If you are really ambitious, you can plan a picnic fair at your school, church, or local park. This project requires more preparation and participation than other fund-raising projects do, but it can be fun and rewarding, both financially and socially.

1. Choose a Saturday during a warm season to have your picnic fair.

2. Get permission from the school or the town to use their property and toilet facilities.

3. Spread the word around town by posters, notices in churches, newsletters, and announcements on local radio.

4. Ask local shops to donate prizes or gift certificates to give the winners of games and contests at your picnic fair.

5. Invite the community to bring their lunches and their blankets to the picnic fair and spend the afternoon getting to know their neighbors.

6. Organize games and activities to make money at the fair. For example, you could have different games of chance, play-off games of tennis or basketball, relay races, talent shows, or scavenger hunts. You could also make homemade ice cream to sell.

7. Maybe a local band would be willing to play at the picnic for a while. It would be good exposure for a band trying to make a name for itself. Just keep the audience in mind. Loud rock music may not be very appealing to parents and grandparents. Ask the band to play easy music that everyone will like.

8. Organize a team of kids to clean up the litter after the picnic fair is over.

Grade Level:	K–12
You Will Need:	A play about caring, props, posters, flyers
Time Required:	12–40 hours

100. Produce a Play

Wouldn't you like to be a producer? You can write and produce a play to benefit a charity project.

1. Writing the play is the most difficult part of this project. It is more fun to write it with a group of kids, with everyone contributing a different character or line to the play. Try to write a story that promotes human kindness and is not violent or insulting to any race, sex, or religion.

2. Choose a date to perform your play, and get permission from your school or city hall to use their auditorium.

3. Make a list of all the props you will need to perform your play and begin collecting them from friends, neighbors, and shop owners.

4. Assign parts in the play to your friends and create a schedule of practices. Ask every actor and actress to commit to the practices.

5. Let the community know about your play by putting wooden sandwich boards on as many street corners as you can, hanging posters all around town and in your school, putting ads on the radio and in the newspaper, and making flyers to put under windshield wipers, to leave in store windows, and to send home with kids in school.

6. If you have access to a copy machine, you can make programs to hand out the night of the play. The program

should include the names of all the actors and actresses, all the stores that contributed props, and information on the charity project that the profits will support.

7. You can charge admission to the play, or you can let people come in for free and then take up a collection during intermission. (If you try the collection idea, you should explain the charity project you are financing during intermission before asking for any money.)

I have included two skits (short plays) that were performed by Kids Care Clubs in Connecticut. Cindy Princi is an actress from New York City who wrote the skits and helped the kids practice and perform them. Both skits were performed with such perfection that the audience thought they were professionals. You can use either of these skits for your production and add another couple of skits, or you can write your own full-length play.

Torn Apart

by
Cindy Princi and the New Canaan Kids Care Club

Cast and Crew
Sam
Benji
Mother
Father
5 Students
Mark (another student)
Teacher/Ms. Windall
Sun (very young child can be used for this part)
Moon (a very young child can be used for this part)
Narrator
Backstage Crew

This play uses a T-shirt to represent the broken hearts of humans. Every time Sam is hurt by someone, she rips her shirt from the bottom to the neck. By the end of the play, her shirt is shredded, but then some things happen that heal her, and she wakes up the next morning with a new shirt which is not ripped. The actor or actress who plays Sam should have three T-shirts. One plain white T-shirt to wear under the others for modesty's sake, and two white T-shirts with large solid hearts drawn on them, one to rip up and one to wear at the conclusion. We found that the T-shirt would rip more easily if three-inch cuts were made in the hem prior to show time.

SCENE ONE—Sam's bedroom

Opens with moon crossing stage (entering the stage from one side and exiting on the other side). Sam is in bed. Sun walks in and stands in corner of room, visible behind Sam.

Alarm clock rings and Sam jumps up and falls out of bed.

Sam throws blankets back on bed and sits dejected on floor. Looks down at T-shirt she is wearing and studies it for a minute, drawing the audience's attention to the shirt. On the shirt is drawn in permanent marker a large solid heart of red or bright pink.

Sam goes off stage and returns wearing jeans and combing her hair. Sam sits on the bed and puts on shoes, but does not tie laces. Sam stands, her back to the bedroom door, and looks into mirror to fix hair.

Enter Benji

BENJI: **Good morning, Sis. Mom has breakfast ready, and everyone is at the table but YOU!**

SAM: **I'm coming, I'm coming. I just got up on the wrong side of the bed. You know? I didn't get a great start.**

Sam returns to fixing her hair in mirror, standing with legs slightly apart.

Benji starts to leave but looks over shoulder and stops (has an idea).

Benji drops to floor and quietly crawls behind Sam and ties Sam's shoelaces together, then scurries out the bedroom door.

Sam finishes her hair and turns to go to breakfast (unaware of laces). Sam falls. Sam sits up, looks at her laces, looks in the direction that Benji ran, stands up, then rips the T-shirt from the hem to the neck in one angry motion. Then walks off stage.

SCENE TWO—the kitchen table

Sam, carrying a stack of papers which is supposed to be a term paper, walks into the kitchen for breakfast.

Sam sits in a chair, happy to be finally catching up, and exhales with a smile.

Everyone else gets up from the table to leave.

MOTHER: **What a shame you weren't able to join us, dear.**

Mother kisses Sam on the head and goes out the door.

Sam watches them leave with mouth half open, looks dejected, and her head drops down to see T-shirt. Sam stands up and rips T-shirt from hem to neck. Sam walks off stage, accidentally leaving the term paper on the table.

SCENE THREE—the school

Students are seated in classroom facing audience; teacher is standing with back to audience. One seat is left in front row, beside Mark.

Sam rushes in with book bag and sits in empty seat in front row.

TEACHER: **Everyone, please hand in your term papers.**

Sam opens her book bag to get her term paper and then remembers she left it on the kitchen table. She looks desperately back to the kitchen set, then sinks in her chair. Meanwhile, the teacher has been collecting papers from the other students. The teacher gets to Sam and holds out her hand for the paper.

SAM: **Oh, Ms. Windall, you just have to believe me! I left my paper on the kitchen table. Really. I wrote it on the subcultural grunge movement among American teenagers. I worked hard. I just left it on—**

MS. WINDALL: (interrupting Sam) **The paper was due this morning. I will not accept late papers. You will get a zero.**

Sam, totally depleted, looks again at her T-shirt and rips it another time. Sam feels someone staring; she turns slowly toward Mark.

Mark is smiling sympathetically. Sam is relieved to be understood. Sam returns his smile.

SCENE FOUR—Sam's bedroom

The sun walks across the stage and then exits, and the moon walks out and takes his place behind Sam's bed.

Sam enters room in flannel pajama bottoms and ripped T-shirt. Sam takes off the ripped T-shirt and throws it in a drawer. (Already in the drawer, unknown to the audience, is the other T-shirt with a heart and no rips.) Sam gets into bed and pulls up covers.

Mother and Father come in.

MOTHER: **I love you, dear. Sleep well.**

FATHER: **Good night, sweetheart, I love you, too.**

Mother and father leave. Sam smiles and snuggles down into her blanket.

Benji comes bolting into the room wearing pajamas and carrying a toothbrush, then he stops by her bed and bends over with his face in hers.

BENJI: **Hey, Sis, sorry about the laces this morning. 'Night.**

Benji exits.

CONCLUSION—Sam's bedroom

Moon walks across the stage and exits. Sun walks onto the stage and stands behind Sam in bed.

Alarm rings.

Sam gets up and walks to dresser.

Slowly she removes her T-shirt and stares in disbelief. It is no longer ripped. She pulls on the fabric and excitedly puts it over her head and stretches the front to view (and draw audience attention to) the heart on the front.

SAM: (now addressing the audience and pointing to her shirt) **I am not torn apart if I am loved. I am whole.**

Entire cast and Narrator step onto stage behind her and together they repeat:

ALL: **I am not torn apart if I am loved. I am whole.**

Narrator, holding the old ripped T-shirt, steps forward from cast and takes stage in front of Sam.

NARRATOR: (holding up the ripped shirt) **Do you know anyone who wears a shirt like this? They are everywhere. You can see them—if you look—in soup kitchens, homeless shelters, your school, your office, maybe even your home. What does it take to put these people back together, to mend their rips and tears? We know what it takes.**

Each cast member steps forward and offers a solution. For example, one might say, "It takes courage." Another might say, *"It takes hope."* Another might say, *"It takes time and caring."* Or someone might say, *"It takes reaching out of ourselves and taking a risk."*

CAST (ONE AT A TIME): It takes _____ (you fill in the blanks).

The Snowman

by
Cindy Princi

Cast
Snowman
Child 1
Child 2
Child 3
Child 4
Child 5
Child 6

SCENE ONE

Snowman dressed in stretchy white clothing with stuffing to look round, sits in a chair in center stage with a stocking over his head.

Children all enter together dressed in winter coats, hats, mittens.

Children are playing and patting the snowman as though they have just finished making him.

ALL CHILDREN: He looks great!

CHILD 1: He needs a hat.

CHILD 2: Yeah, and a corncob pipe.

CHILD 3: I have a scarf at home that would look great on him.

CHILD 4: I have a pair of boots.

CHILD 5: I have an old jacket that he could wear.

ALL CHILDREN: Let's go get them!

All children run off stage except Child 6. Child 6 stays on stage and pats the snowman some more. He seems to be thinking.

SCENE TWO

After a few minutes, the children all return with the items they got for the snowman. Each child puts his or her item on the snowman and then backs up.

ALL CHILDREN: He looks great!

CHILD 1: I can't wait until Christmas. I'm going to get a _____.

(Let the actors and actresses playing these roles fill in the biggest, best toy they can think of—a different toy for each child.)

CHILD 2: I want a _____ for Christmas.

CHILD 3: I want a _____.

CHILD 4: I want a big _____ for Christmas.

CHILD 5: I want a _____.

Child 5 turns to Child 6

CHILD 5: Well, what do you want for Christmas?

CHILD 6: I want there to be no more hungry children in the world, and no more homeless children in the world.

ALL CHILDREN: But that's no present!

CHILD 6: It is to all those kids who don't have any food to eat, and to all those babies who don't have any place to sleep.

All the children look down at the ground, then slowly begin to look at one another. They all seem to have the same idea at the same time.

CHILD 1: **Let's take this stuff to the homeless shelter.**

CHILD 2: **Yeah, the kids there need this stuff more than the snowman does.**

The children grab the clothing they had put on the snowman and run off stage to the shelter. Only the corncob pipe is left in the snowman's mouth.

Child 6 is alone on stage with the snowman. He or she walks over to the snowman, looking a little sad. He then grabs the corncob from the snowman's mouth and runs after the other children.

CHILD 6: **Hey! Wait for me!**

Grade Level:	2–12
You Will Need:	Lunch foods, bags, napkins, cash box, change, signs, display table
Time Required:	2–8 hours

101. Sell Bag Lunches

Lunches are a big business. Every working adult, every teacher, and almost every student eats lunch away from home. Many restaurants are in business for their lunch business alone. You can capitalize on the lunch industry by selling bag lunches.

1. You can make vegetarian lunch bags (with no animal products), or health-nut lunch bags (low salt, low fat, etc.), or

junk-food lunch bags (need I describe?), or sports-jock lunch bags (high in protein and carbohydrates), or any other type of lunch that you think would sell for a profit.

2. Get permission to sell your lunch bags at school during lunch break to students and teachers.

3. During the summer you can get permission from your town or city to sell lunch bags downtown where local businesspeople can buy them.

4. Price the lunch bags according to what the market will bear. Find out what the competition charges and charge less.

5. Start small, with only a few lunches. As you sell them, you can make more.

6. A more complex version of this project is to get permission from your school to open a lunch bar. In our high school the kids have many lunch choices, but there is not much available for students who are health or diet conscious. (There is also no pizza!) Think about what your school is lacking in lunch choices and set up a lunch bar to serve it. This project can provide an ongoing revenue source for your Kids Care Club. In fact, your Kids Care Club can operate the lunch bar together, taking turns working at lunch break and shopping for supplies.

Grade Level:	K–12
You Will Need:	Fabric and sewing materials
Time Required:	2–10 hours

102. Care Quilt Raffle

In years past, groups of women got together once a week to create beautiful quilts. Perhaps the quilt would be for one of the women in the quilting circle, or perhaps they would donate it to a church raffle.

1. You and your friends can meet weekly and talk or listen to music while you make a quilt to sell for profit. The profit could be used to finance a charity project you plan to do together.

2. Making a quilt is more complicated than this page will allow. There are books in the library that explain the process better. You may also know someone who has made quilts before and would be willing to teach you and your friends.

3. Quilts are made by sewing squares of different fabric together in a pattern. You can make a small baby quilt, using pastel fabrics with childlike designs, or you can make a king-size quilt using floral, striped, and bold fabrics.

4. After the squares are all sewn together, you can attach a one-piece backing made of cotton or flannel. The backing is stitched to the front on all four sides. Yarn is threaded through the back and front in many places on the quilt and tied in knots to hold the pieces securely together. Blanket binding or some other fabric can be attached to the edges to hide the rough ends.

5. You can make more money by raffling your quilt than by selling it to one buyer. You can make raffle tickets from index cards cut into three pieces. Write a number on the two corners of each raffle ticket, a different number for each ticket. List all the numbers on a piece of paper, which you can call your ticket log. As you sell raffle tickets, you will record the name and phone number of the buyer on the ticket log beside the number of the ticket purchased. Tear the ticket in half and give one half to the buyer, and put the other half in a jar to be used for the drawing. (Make sure the number is printed clearly on each half.)

6. You can sell raffle tickets to your friends, neighbors, church members, family, and teachers.

7. Display the quilt in the library or school office with a poster that explains who made the quilt and what charity it will benefit. Also give the date of the drawing.

8. On the day of the drawing, ask a young child to reach inside the jar and choose a ticket. You should be able to locate the winner by looking up the number of the winning ticket on the ticket log.

Grade Level:	5–12
You Will Need:	Wrapping paper, tape, ribbons, bows, table, scissors, cash box, change, display signs
Time Required:	4–40 hours

103. Gift Wrapping

This is a great fund-raising project for the Christmas season, when many people are shopping for gifts. Weary shoppers would appreciate taking a rest and letting you do the wrapping for them.

1. This project is most successfully accomplished in a mall, shopping plaza, or a large department store. You will have to get permission from the manager to set up your gift-wrapping service. Managers are not likely to refuse if you tell them what charity your profits will be used for, unless some other charitable organization has already asked for permission to do the same thing. You should request permission as early as possible (even June) to be sure someone else doesn't get there first.

2. If some other organization is wrapping gifts in the mall

or store that you choose, ask if you can wrap in the evenings only.

3. After you have permission to wrap gifts in a mall or store, you will need to collect wrapping paper of various patterns, a long, sturdy table, scissors, tape, ribbons, and bows.

4. Make two or three display signs from posterboard. Allow yourself and your friends enough time to be creative and careful with your posters; they will attract or put off your customers. The posters should say in bold print GIFT WRAPPING, and you should also list the price you will charge (you might want to charge by the size of the package) and the charity the profit will benefit. Decorate the posters to make them attractive, perhaps outlining the posters with samples of the paper you will be using.

5. You can buy the paper and keep the receipts so that the first profits pay you back for your investment, or you can ask the students and parents in your school or church to donate wrapping paper to your cause.

6. This activity requires a few kids to be available to wrap gifts at the same time (you might have lines of customers waiting). Before the gift wrapping starts, you should make a schedule of who will work on which days and for how many hours. Tell kids that they are responsible for finding someone else to cover for them if they can't make it.

7. At the end of each shift, one person should be in charge of the cash box. You can determine how much change should remain in the cash box (post it on the lid of the box, for example, 50¢ in pennies, $2 in nickels, etc.), and the rest of the money is profit. Choose a place where profits from each shift should be dropped off.

8. Remind all the wrappers that this project is for a charitable cause and that they should not wrap gifts for friends or family without charging them, or they will be taking the profits from your charity project.

9. You can begin your gift-wrapping service as early as November. Many people begin their shopping early. But the most profitable time will be the two weeks before Christmas, when last-minute shoppers are looking for all the help they can get.

Note: An adult should be present at the wrapping table at all times to supervise and protect the kids from the dangers that exist in any large group of strangers.

Grade Level:	6–12
You Will Need:	Tickets, posters, flyers, large jug, one prize, awards, cash box, change
Time Required:	4–20 hours

104. Benefit Games

A benefit game is any event where ticket sales are used to benefit a charity project. Most benefit games are arranged with comedy and fun in mind, versus a game between two professional teams. In Connecticut, the radio personalities at WPLJ radio (a popular station for teens) challenged the faculty at New Canaan High School to a softball game which would benefit a little girl with cancer. The rock star Meatloaf and World Wrestling star Sergeant Slaughter also volunteered to play. They raised $20,000 to help pay the little girl's medical costs. Radio personalities are often willing to participate in benefit games, and students are happy to buy a ticket to watch their favorite radio host play a sport. Also, professional sports teams may be willing to play the teachers, or the local police officers and firefighters, or the cheerleaders at your school.

1. You can arrange a benefit game that would be attractive to students in your school district. The first step is to contact the players and ask them to play.

2. Set a date for the game which both teams agree to (or maybe you will have more than two teams, like a play-off). Make sure it is far enough in advance to allow plenty of time for advertising.

3. Start advertising the game using radio (if one of the teams is from a radio station, they will give you a lot of free advertising), local and school newspapers, posters everywhere, flyers, and announcements at school, and you can set up little tables outside of stores to sell tickets.

4. You can also start a side game to get kids talking about the benefit game, by placing a big jug in the school lobby and inviting kids to guess what the final score will be. Offer some great prize, like dinner with the cheerleaders or football team, or an autographed radio, or something you think is funny.

5. Try to think of halftime entertainment too. Maybe the football team would dress like cheerleaders and perform a few funny cheers for the crowd.

6. During halftime you can make a little more money by selling cookies, brownies, chips, sodas, etc.

7. Make sure that you and all the kids who organized the benefit game present the participating teams with awards, trophies, blue ribbons, school hats, or something that lets them know that you appreciate their time and effort.

8. The prize for the guessing game and the awards for the teams can be donated by local stores or businesses.

9. You can create a program to hand out at the gate which explains the charity project you hope to finance with the profits from the game, and lists the names of the participating team members as well as the names of any stores or individuals who donated items to the event.

Grade Level:	2–12
You Will Need:	Several different types of candy bars, notepaper, tape, posterboard, string
Time Required:	1–4 hours

105. Candy Telegrams

This project is easy, a lot of fun, and spreads good feelings all over the school. I first saw this project in Saxe Middle School in New Canaan, Connecticut. Kids were carrying around candy bars and notepaper, which other kids could buy for fifty cents each. However, the buyer didn't eat the candy bar, but sent it with a telegram (message written on the notepaper), to another kid in the school. The kids loved it, and they sold many candy telegrams.

1. The first step is to get permission from the principal to sell candy bars during lunch, recess, or after school.

2. Buy or ask local stores to donate candy bars of various flavors but about the same size.

3. Decide on a price for the candy telegram that covers the cost of the candy and allows for some profit.

4. Cut several large pieces of posterboard in half and write CANDY TELEGRAMS in large bold letters on them; also write the price you will charge. Make holes in the upper left-hand and upper righthand corner of each poster. Using two pieces of string, attach two posters together with the blank sides inside and the written sides out. The strings serve as shoulder straps, so you need to leave about ten inches of slack in each string. The posters can be slipped over the head and

worn like a billboard by the kids who are selling candy telegrams around school.

5. Each time a kid buys a candy telegram, you should be told to whom it goes, and the buyer should write a short message on the notepaper which you tape to the candy bar. You deliver the candy bar and the message to the student or teacher it is purchased for.

APPENDIX I

Social Organizations/ Volunteer Opportunities

How to Find a Social Organization

The following section contains names and addresses of social service organizations which offer various types of assistance to people with needs. The organizations are listed by their charity focus: the poor, the children, the elderly, the handicapped, or injustice. Some organizations are listed several times because they help several groups of people.

Also included in the section entitled Organizations That Help the Poor is a state-by-state directory of homeless coalitions. These are a good resource for finding the names of homeless shelters and soup kitchens in your area.

Your phone book is another good source of social service organizations.

Be Patient

When we first began to look for ways that kids could help others, we sent out fifty service request forms to local human service organizations. Only two were returned, and they wanted the kids to stuff envelopes. Disappointed but not defeated, we began to develop our own projects, which became the bulk of this book. Four years later, as my research assistant, Jenny, called the following organizations to verify addresses, she also asked if they had specific ways that kids could volunteer to help their cause. The positive response was not overwhelming. While many organizations wanted the kids to earn money for them or do clerical work, only two suggested meaningful ways that kids could participate in their organization. Things change slowly.

I do not tell you this to discourage you from calling these organizations. On the contrary, please call them. But don't be impatient if you speak to some organizations that are seemingly apathetic to the involvement of kids, and some that are downright opposed. Every request they receive on behalf of the kids will bring them a step closer to recognizing the gold mine of youth they have been ignoring. The kids are their own best testimony.

Organizations That Help the Poor

American National Red Cross
431 D St., N.W.
Washington, DC 20006
(202) 737-8300

AmeriCares
161 Cherry St.
New Canaan, CT 06840
(203) 966-5195
(800) 666-HOPE

CARE USA
660 First Ave.
New York, NY 10016
(212) 686-3110
(800) 242-GIVE

Catholic Charities
1319 F St., N.W.
Washington, DC 20004
(202) 526-4100

CHILDHELP USA
6463 Independence Ave.
Woodland Hills, CA 91367
(818) 347-7280

Children's Aide International
Box 83220
San Diego, CA 92138-3220
(213) 519-8923
(800) 842-2810

Christian Children's Fund
P.O. Box 85066
Richmond, VA 23286
(800) 776-6767

Coalition for the Homeless
105 E. 22nd. St.
New York, NY 10010
(212) 460-8110

Covenant House
346 W. 17th St.
New York, NY 10011
(212) 727-4000
(800) 922-6465

Food Industry Crusade Against
   Hunger
800 Connecticut Ave., N.W.
Washington, DC 20006
(202) 429-4555

The Freedom From Hunger
   Foundation
P.O. Box 95617
Davis, CA 95616
(916) 758-6200

The Fresh Air Fund
1040 Sixth Ave.
New York, NY 10018
(212) 221-0900

Goodwill Industries of America, Inc.
9200 Wisconsin Ave.
Bethesda, MD 20814
(301) 530-6500

Habitat for Humanity
121 Habitat St.
Americus, GA 31709
(912) 924-6935

Hole in the Wall Gang Camp Fund
555 Long Wharf Drive
New Haven, CT 06511
(203) 772-0522

Interagency Council on the Homeless
451 Seventh St., S.W.
Washington, DC 20410
(202) 708-1480

Maryknoll Fathers
P.O. Box 301
Maryknoll, NY 10545-0301

Maryknoll Fathers
Father Peter LeJacq
BUGANDO P.O. 1421
Mwanza, Tansania

National Alliance to End
    Homelessness
1518 K St., N.W., Suite 206
Washington, DC 20005
(202) 638-1526

National Coalition for the Homeless
1612 K St., N.W., #1004
Washington, DC 20006-2802
(202) 775-1322

National Student Campaign Against
    Hunger
29 Temple Place
Boston, MA 02111
(617) 292-4823

Neighbor to Neighbor
2601 Mission St., Suite 400
San Francisco, CA 94110
(415) 824-3355

Points of Light Foundation
1737 H St., N.W.
Washington, DC 20006
(800) 879-5400

Prison Fellowship
P.O. Box 17500
Washington, DC 20041

Salvation Army
P.O. Box 269
Alexandria, VA 22313
(703) 684-5500

Second Harvest, National Food Bank
116 S. Michigan Ave., Suite 4
Chicago, IL 60603
(312) 263-2303

Trevor's Campaign for the Homeless
3415 Westchester Pike
Newtown Square, PA 19073
(215) 325-0640

Weingart Center Meal Coupon
    Program
515 East Sixth St.
Los Angeles, CA 90021
(213) 622-3629

World SHARE
5255 Lovelock St.
San Diego, CA 92110
(619) 294-2981

State-by-State Directory of Coalitions That Serve the Homeless

(Produced by the National Coalition for the Homeless [see listing above]. You can contact the National Coalition at (202) 775-1322.)

Alabama
The Alabama Coalition for the
    Homeless
2101 W. Daniel Payne Dr.
Birmingham, AL 35214
(205) 791-2040

Alabama Low-Income Housing
P.O. Box 95
Epes, AL 35460
(205) 652-9676

Alaska
Alaska Coalition for the Homeless
P.O. Box 75286
Fairbanks, AK 99707
(907) 456-3876

Arizona
Arizona Coalition to End
  Homelessness
P.O. Box 933
Phoenix, AZ 85001-0933
(602) 258-7201

Arkansas
Arkansas Coalition for the Prevention
  of Homelessness
P.O. Box 164009
Little Rock, AR 72216
(501) 374-1748

Arkansas Low-Income Housing
400 W. Markham
Little Rock, AR 72201
(501) 324-9255

California
California Homeless & Housing
  Coalition
926 J St., #422
Sacramento, CA 95814
(916) 447-0390

California Homeless & Housing
  Coalition
Southern California Branch
1010 S. Flower St., #500
Los Angeles, CA 90015
(213) 746-7690

Colorado
Colorado Affordable Housing
  Partnership
1981 Blake St.
Denver, CO 80202-1272
(303) 297-2548

Colorado Coalition for the Homeless
2100 Broadway
Denver, CO 80205
(303) 293-2217

Connecticut
Connecticut Coalition to End
  Homelessness
30 Jordon Lane
Wethersfield, CT 06109
(203) 721-7876

Delaware
Delaware Housing Coalition
P.O. Box 1633
Dover, DE 19903-1633
(302) 678-2286

Delaware Task Force on
  Homelessness
P.O. Box 1653
Dover, DE 19903-1653
(302) 674-8500

District of Columbia
Coalition of Housing & Homeless
  Organizations
1700 Pennsylvania Ave., N.W.,
  #800
Washington, DC 20006
(202) 639-3804

Florida
Florida Coalition for the Homeless
119 Ferndale Dr.
Tallahassee, FL 32302
(904) 878-1239

Georgia
Georgia Homeless Resource Network
363 Georgia Ave., S.E.
Atlanta, GA 30312
(404) 230-5008

Georgia Housing Coalition
615 Peachtree St., N.E., #1130
Atlanta, GA 30308
(404) 892-4824

Hawaii
Affordable Housing Alliance
2331 Seaview Ave.
P.O. Box 1329
Honolulu, HI 96807-1329
(808) 946-2244

Hawaii Statewide Coalition for the
    Homeless
277 Ohua Ave.
Honolulu, HI 96815
(808) 922-4787

Homeless Aloha, Inc.
1002 N. School St., Bldg. H
Honolulu, HI 96817
(808) 848-8801

Idaho
Idaho Housing Coalition
P.O. Box 1805
Boise, ID 83701
(208) 338-7066

Illinois
Chicago Coalition to End
    Homelessness
1325 S. Wabash St., #205
Chicago, IL 60605
(312) 435-0225

Illinois Coalition to End
    Homelessness
522 East Monroe St., #304
Springfield, IL 62701
(217) 788-8060

Statewide Housing Action Coalition
202 S. State St., #1414
Chicago, IL 60604
(312) 939-6074

Indiana
Hoosier Valley Coalition for Housing
    and Homeless Issues
P.O. Box 843
Jeffersonville, IN 47130
(812) 288-6451

Indiana Coalition for Housing and
    Homeless Issues
902 N. Capital Ave.
Indianapolis, IN 46204
(317) 636-8819

Iowa
Iowa Coalition for Housing and the
    Homeless
921 Pleasant St., #111
Des Moines, IA 50309-2698
(515) 288-5022

Kentucky
Homeless & Housing Coalition of
    Kentucky
3407 Rowena Rd., #2
Louisville, KY 40218-1341
(502) 589-6488

Louisiana
Louisiana Coalition for the Homeless
Orleans Parish School System
4100 Touro St.
New Orleans, LA 70122
(504) 286-2884

Louisiana for Low-Income Housing
    Today
P.O. Box 50100
New Orleans, LA 70150-0100
(504) 943-0044

Maine
Maine Coalition for the Homeless
P.O. Box 415
Augusta, ME 04332
(207) 626-3567

Maryland
Action for the Homeless
1021 N. Calvert
Baltimore, MD 21202-3823
(410) 659-0300

Maryland Low-Income Housing
Coalition
28 E. Ostend
Baltimore, MD 21230
(410) 727-4200

Massachusetts
Massachusetts Affordable Housing
Alliance
25 West St., 3rd floor
Boston, MA 02111
(617) 728-9100

Massachusetts Coalition for the
Homeless
288 A St., 4th floor
Boston, MA 02210
(617) 737-3508

Massachusetts Shelter Providers
Association
701 Main Street
P.O. Box 17078
Worcester, MA 01601
(508) 753-2271

Michigan
Michigan Coalition Against
Homelessness
1210 W. Saginaw
Lansing, MI 48915
(517) 377-0509

Minnesota
Minnesota Coalition for the
Homeless
122 W. Franklin Ave., #318
Minneapolis, MN 55404
(612) 870-7073

Mississippi
Mississippi Housing Coalition
P.O. Box 1898
Hattiesburg, MS 39403-1898
(601) 545-4595

Mississippi United Against
Homelessness
P.O. Box 905
Meridian, MS 39302
(601) 483-4838

Missouri
Missouri Association for Social
Welfare
308 E. High St.
Jefferson City, MO 63110
(314) 634-2901

Montana
Montana People's Action
208 E. Main St.
Missoula, MT 59802
(406) 728-5297

Montana Low-Income Coalition
P.O. Box 1029
Helena, MT 59624
(406) 449-8801

Nevada
Nevada State Homeless Coalition
P.O. Box 8297
Incline Village, NV 89452
(702) 687-4170

New Hampshire
New Hampshire Coalition for the
Homeless
1039 Auburn St.
Manchester, NH 03103
(603) 623-4888

New Jersey
Non-Profit Affordable Housing
Network of New Jersey
P.O. Box 1746
Trenton, NJ 08607
(609) 393-3752

Right to Housing Coalition of New
  Jersey
118 Division St.
Elizabeth, NJ 07201
(908) 352-2989

New Mexico
New Mexico Coalition to End
  Homelessness
P.O. Box 25141
Albuquerque, NM 87125
(505) 247-3361

New York
New York Rural Housing Coalition
350 Northern Blvd., #101
Albany, NY 12204
(518) 434-1314

New York State Coalition for the
  Homeless
235 Lark St.
Albany, NY 12210
(518) 436-5612

North Carolina
North Carolina Low-Income Housing
  Coalition
P.O. Box 27863
Raleigh, NC 27611-7863
(919) 833-6201

North Dakota
North Dakota Coalition for Homeless
  People
401 Third Ave. N.
Fargo, ND 58102
(701) 241-1360

Ohio
Ohio Coalition for the Homeless
1066 N. High Street
Columbus, OH 43201-2440
(614) 291-1984

Ohio Rural Housing
P.O. Box 787
Athens, OH 45701
(614) 594-8499

Oklahoma
Oklahoma Homeless Network
P.O. Box 400
Norman, OK 73070
(405) 360-5100

Oregon
Oregon Housing Now
2710 N.E. 14th St.
Portland, OR 97212

Oregon Shelter Network, Inc.
2211 Eleventh St.
Tillamook, OR 97141
(503) 842-5261

Pennsylvania
Pennsylvania Low-Income Housing
2 Gateway Center
Pittsburg, PA 15222
(412) 281-2102

Puerto Rico
Coalition for the Right of the
  Homeless
Montebello A-O
Garden Hills, PR 00966
(809) 724-4051

Rhode Island
Rhode Island Housing Network
P.O. Box 23188
Providence, RI 02903-3188
(401) 351-8719

Rhode Island Coalition for the
  Homeless
102 Linwood Ave.
Providence, RI 02907
(401) 421-6458

Rhode Island Right to Housing
Amos House
P.O. Box 2873
Providence, RI 02907
(401) 272-0220

Statewide Housing Action Coalition
Rhode Island Housing Agency
60 Eddy St.
Providence, RI 02903
(401) 751-5566

South Carolina
South Carolina Citizens for Housing
P.O. Box 86
Columbia, SC 29202
(803) 734-6122

South Carolina Coalition for the
   Homeless
3425 N. Main St.
Columbia, SC 29203
(803) 779-4706

South Carolina Low-Income Housing
   Coalition
Marvin Lane
P.O. Box 1520
Columbia, SC 29202
(803) 734-6122

South Dakota
Sioux Falls Homeless Coalition
P.O. Box 1643
Sioux Falls, SD 57101
(605) 335-4217

Tennessee
Tennessee Housing & Homeless
   Coalition
2012 21st Ave., S.
Nashville, TN 37212
(615) 385-2221

Texas
Texas Alliance for Human Needs
2520 Longview, #311
Austin, TX 78705
(512) 474-5019

Texas Homeless Network
411 W. Second St.
Austin, TX 78701
(512) 478-9971

Texas Low-Income Housing
   Information Service
1100 East Eighth St.
Austin, TX 78702
(512) 477-8910

Utah
Utah Homeless Coordinating Council
Utah Issues
1385 W. Indiana
Salt Lake City, UT 84104
(801) 521-2025

Utah Housing Coalition
50 S. Main St., #2007
Salt Lake City, UT 84103-0815
(801) 535-1258

Vermont
Vermont Affordable Housing
P.O. Box 827
Montpelier, VT 05602
(802) 223-1448

Vermont Coalition for the Homeless
P.O. Box 1616
Burlington, VT 05402
(802) 864-7402

Virgin Islands
Interfaith Coalition of St. Croix
P.O. Box 88
Frederiksted
St. Croix, VI 00841
(809) 772-1142

Virginia
Virginia Coalition for the Homeless
7825 Cherokee Rd.
Richmond, VA 23225
(804) 320-4577

Virginia Housing Coalition
P.O. Box 8
Onancock, VA 23417
(804) 787-3532

Washington
Housing Trust Fund Coalition
P.O. Box 31151
Seattle, WA 98103
(206) 634-2222

Washington State Coalition for the
  Homeless
P.O. Box 955
Tacoma, WA 98401
(206) 572-4237

Washington Low-Income Housing
  Congress
315 W. Mission Ave.
Spokane, WA 99201-2341
(509) 325-0755

Washington Low-Income Housing
  Network
107 Pine St., #103
Seattle, WA 98101
(206) 442-9455

West Virginia
West Virginia Housing Coalition
P.O. Box 987
Elkins, WV 26241
(304) 636-5897

Wisconsin
Wisconsin Coalition to End
  Homelessness
807 N. East Ave.
Waukesha, WI 53186
(414) 549-8720

Wisconsin Partnership for Housing
123 E. Main St.
Madison, WI 53705
(608) 258-5560

Wyoming
Wyoming Against Homelessness
930 Western Hills Blvd.
Cheyenne, WY 82009
(307) 637-8634
(307) 635-9261

Organizations That Help the Children

ACTION Drug Alliance
1100 Vermont Ave., N.W.
Washington, DC 20525
(202) 606-4857

ALSAC St. Jude Children's Research
  Hospital
501 St. Jude Place
Memphis, TN 38105
(901) 522-9733
(800) USS-JUDE

A Better Chance
419 Boylston St.
Boston, MA 02116
(617) 421-0950

Big Brothers/Big Sisters
230 N. 13th St.
Philadelphia, PA 19107
(215) 567-7000

Boys And Girls Clubs Of America
771 First Ave.
New York, NY 10017
(212) 351-5900

A Chance to Grow
3700 Bryant Ave., N.
Minneapolis, MN 55412
(612) 521-2266

Child Find of America
7 Innis Ave.
New Paltz, NY 12561
(914) 255-1848

CHILDHELP USA
6463 Independence Ave.
Woodland Hills, CA 91367
(818) 347-7280

Children's Aide International
Box 83220
San Diego, CA 92138-3220
(213) 519-8923
(800) 842-2810

Children's Defense Fund
25 E. St., N.W.
Washington, DC 20001
(202) 628-8787

Christian Children's Fund
P.O. Box 85066
Richmond, VA 23286
(800) 776-6767

Covenant House
346 W. 17th St.
New York, NY 10011
(212) 727-4000
(800) 922-6465

Creative Resource Center
1103 Forest Ave.
Portland, Maine 04103
(207) 797-9543

Federation for Children With Special
   Needs
95 Berkeley St., Suite 104
Boston, MA 02116
(617) 482-2915

Fresh Air Fund
1040 Sixth Ave.
New York, NY 10018
(212) 221-0900

Generations United
Child Welfare League of America
440 First St., Suite 310
Washington, DC 20001-2085
(202) 638-2952

Hole in the Wall Gang Camp Fund
555 Long Wharf Drive
New Haven, CT 06511
(203) 772-0522

Just Say No International
2101 Webster St., Suite 1300
Oakland, CA 94612
(800) 258-2766

Kids Against Crime
1700 Northeast St.
San Bernardino, CA 92405
(909) 882-1344

Kids Care Clubs
P.O. Box 1083
New Canaan, CT 06840

Leaders for Literacy
Reading Is Fundamental
Smithsonian Institute
600 Maryland Ave., S.W., Suite 600
Washington, DC 20024-2520
(202) 287-3220

Mail for Tots
25 New Charndon St.
P.O. Box 8699
Boston, MA 02114

Make a Wish Foundation
100 W. Clarendon, Suite 2200
Phoenix, AZ 85013-3518
(800) 722-WISH

National Association of Child
   Advocates
1625 K Street, N.W., Suite 510
Washington, DC 20006
(202) 828-6950

National Association of State
   Coordinators for the Education of
   Homeless Children
1710 N. Congress Ave.
Austin, TX 78758
(512) 463-9067

National Center for Missing and
   Exploited Children
1835 K. St., N.W., Suite 600
Washington, DC 20006
(703) 235-3900

National Child Abuse Hotline
(800) 4 A CHILD

National Children's Cancer Society
18 Lindenwood Dr.
Troy, IL 62294
(618) 667-9563

National Committee for the
   Prevention of Child Abuse
332 S. Michigan Ave., Suite 11600
Chicago, IL 60604
(312) 663-3520

National Network of Youth and
   Runaway Service
1319 F Street, N.W., Suite 401
Washington, DC 20004
(202) 783-7949

National Runaway Switchboard
3080 N. Lincoln Ave.
Chicago, IL 60657
(312) 880-9860

National Safe Kids Campaign
111 Michigan Ave., N.W.
Washington, DC 20010
(202) 939-4993

Pediatric AIDS Foundation
1311 Colorado Ave.
Santa Monica, CA 90404
(310) 395-9051

Points of Light Foundation
1737 H St., N.W.
Washington, DC 20006
(800) 879-5400

Save the Children
54 Wilton Rd.
Westport, CT 06880
(203) 221-4000

Shriners' Hospital for Crippled
   Children
P.O. Box 31356
Tampa, FL 33631-3356
(813) 281-0300
(800) 237-5055

Special Olympics International
   Headquarters
1350 New York Ave., N.W.,
   Suite 500
Washington, DC 20005
(202) 628-3630

Sunshine Foundation
2001 Bridge St.
Philadelphia, PA 19124
(215) 335-2622

United Nations Children's Fund
UNICEF
3 United Nations Plaza
New York, NY 10017
(212) 326-7000

Youth Build
58 Day St.
Summerville, MA 02144
(617) 623-9900

Organizations That Help the Elderly

Alzheimer's Association
919 N. Michigan Ave.
Chicago, IL 60611-1676
(800) 272-3900

American Association of Homes for
the Aging
529 14th St., N.W.
Washington, DC 20004

Generations United
Child Welfare League
440 First St., Suite 310
Washington, DC 20001-2085
(202) 638-2952

International Senior Citizens
Association
11753 Wilshire Blvd.
Los Angeles, CA 90025

Meals on Wheels
Retired Senior Volunteer Program
1100 Vermont Ave., N.W.
Washington, DC 20525
(202) 606-4851

National Caucus on the Black Aged
1725 DeSales St., N.W.
Washington, DC 20036

National Council on the Aging
1828 L St., N.W., Suite 504
Washington, DC 20036
(202) 479-1200

Points of Light Foundation
1737 H St., N.W.
Washington, DC 20006
(800) 879-5400

Nursing Homes
Senior Centers
Retirement Communities
in your area

Organizations That Help Persons With Handicaps

Alexander Graham Bell
Association for the Deaf
3417 Volta Place N.W.
Washington, DC 20007

American Athletic Association for
the Deaf
1052 Darling St.
Ogden, UT 84403

American Cancer Society
2200 Lake Blvd.
Atlanta, GA 30319
(404) 816-7800
(800)ACS-2345

American Council of the Blind
818 18th St., N.W., Suite 700
Washington, DC 20006

American Foundation for AIDS
 Research
5900 Wilshire Blvd., 23rd. floor
Los Angeles, CA 90036
(213) 857-5900
(212) 719-0033

American Foundation for the Blind
15 W. 16th St.
New York, NY 10011
(212) 620-2000
(800) 232-5463

American Heart Association
7272 Greenville Ave.
Dallas TX 75231
(214) 373-6300

American Lung Association
1740 Broadway
New York, NY 10019
(212) 315-8700

American National Red Cross
431 D St., N.W.
Washington, DC 20006
(202) 737-8300
(800) LUNG USA

American Speech and Hearing
 Association
9030 Old Georgetown Rd.
Bethesda, MD 20014

Aspira of America
1112 16th St., N.W., Suite 340
Washington, DC 20036
(202) 835-3600

Association for Persons With Severe
 Handicaps
11201 Greenwood Ave., N.
Seattle, WA 98133
(206) 361-8870

Braille Insititute of America, Inc.
741 N. Vermont Ave.
Los Angeles, CA 90029
(213) 663-1111

Catholic Charities
1319 F St., N.W.
Washington, DC 20004
(202) 526-4100

Cystic Fibrosis Foundation
6931 Arlington Rd., #200
Bethesda, MD 20814
(301) 951-4422

Dept. of Health, Education and
 Welfare
Bureau for Education of
 Handicapped
330 Independence Ave., S.W.
Washington, DC 20201

Disability Rights, Education and
 Defense Fund
2212 Sixth St.
Berkeley, CA 94710
(510) 644-2555

Epilepsy Foundation of America
4351 Garden City Dr., Suite 406
Landover, MD 20785
(301) 459-3700
(800) EFA-1000

Federation for Children With Special
 Needs
95 Berkely St., Suite 104
Boston, MA 02116
(617) 482-2915

Goodwill Industries of America, Inc.
9200 Wisconsin Ave.
Bethesda, MD 20814
(301) 530-6500

Learning Disabilities Association of
    America
4156 Library Rd.
Pittsburg, PA 15234
(412) 341-1515

Make a Wish Foundation of America
100 W. Clarendon, Suite 2200
Phoenix, AZ 85013-3518
(800) 722-WISH

March of Dimes
1275 Mamaroneck Ave.
White Plains, NY 10605
(914) 428-7100

National AIDS Network
1012 14th St., N.W.
Washington, DC 20005
(202) 347-0390

National Cancer Care Foundation
1180 Ave. of the Americas
New York, NY 10036
(212) 221-3300

National Center for Learning
    Disabilities
99 Park Ave.
New York, NY 10016
(212) 687-7211

National Children's Cancer Society
18 Lindenwood Dr.
Troy, IL 62294
(618) 667-9563

National Easter Seal Society
70 Lake St.
Chicago, IL 60601
(312) 726-6200

North American Riding for the
    Handicapped Association, Inc.
P.O. Box 33150
Denver, CO 80233

Pediatric AIDS Foundation
1311 Colorado Ave.
Santa Monica, CA 90404
(310) 395-9051

Pegasus
(see North American Riding for the
    Handicapped Assoc., Inc.)

Points of Light Foundation
1737 H St., N.W.
Washington, DC 20006
(800) 879-5400

Reading Is Fundamental
Smithsonian Institute
600 Maryland Ave. S.W., Suite 600
Washington, DC 20024-2520
(202) 287-3220

Recording for the Blind
20 Roszel Rd.
Princeton, NJ 08540
(609) 452-0606
(800) 221-4792

Salvation Army
P.O. Box 269
Alexandria, VA 22313
(703) 684-5500

Shriners' Hospital for Crippled
    Children
P.O. Box 31356
Tampa, FL 33631-3356
(813) 281-0300
(800) 237-5055

Special Olympics International
    Headquarters
1350 New York Ave., N.W.
    Suite 500
Washington, DC 20005
(202) 628-3630

Sunburst National AIDS Project
P.O. Box 2824
Petaluma, CA 94952
(707) 769-0169

United States Association for Blind
  Athletes
33 North Institute Street
West Hall, Suite 15
Colorado Springs, CO 80903
(719) 630-0422

Sunshine Foundation
2001 Bridge St..
Philadelphia, PA 19124
(215) 335-2622

U.S. Committee for UNICEF
333 East 38th St.
New York, NY 10016
(212) 686-5522

Organizations That Raise Guide Dogs

Eye Dog Foundation for the Blind
512 North Larchmont Blvd.
Los Angeles, CA 90004
(213) 468-8856

International Guiding Eyes
13445 Glen Oaks Blvd.
Sylmar, CA 91347
(818) 362-5834

Eye of the Pacific Guide Dogs
747 Amana Street 407
Honolulu, Hawaii 96814
(808) 941-1088

Kansas Specialty Dog Service
124 W. Seventh, P.O. Box 216
Washington, KS 66968
(913) 325-2256

Guide Dog Foundation for the Blind
371 East Jericho Turnpike
Smithtown, NY 11787
(516) 265-2121

Leader Dogs for the Blind
1039 S. Rochester Rd.
Rochester, Michigan 48307
(313) 651-9011

Guide Dogs for the Blind
P.O. Box 151200
San Rafael, CA 94915
(415) 499-4000

Seeing Eye Inc.
Washington Valley Rd.
Morristown, NJ 07960
(201) 539-4425

Guiding Dogs for the Blind
611 Granite Spring Rd.
Yorktown Heights, NY 10598
(914) 245-4024

Sidelco Guide Dog Foundation
P.O. Box 142
Bloomfield, CT 06002
(203) 243-5200

Guide Dogs of the Desert
P.O. Box 1692
Palm Springs, CA 92263
(619) 329-6257

Southeastern Guide Dogs
4210 77th St., E.
Palmetto, FL 34221
(813) 729-5665

Organizations That Fight Injustice

American Refugee Committee
2344 Nicollet Ave. S., Suite 350
Minneapolis, MN 55404
(612) 872-7060

Amnesty International
322 Eighth Ave.
New York, NY 10001
(212) 807-8400

Child Find of America
7 Innis Ave.
New Paltz, NY 12561
(914) 255-1848

Children's Defense Fund
25 E. Street, N.W.
Washington, DC 20001
(202) 628-8787

Just Say No International
2101 Webster St., Suite 1300
Oakland, CA 94612

Kids Against Crime
1700 Northeast St.
San Bernardino, CA 92405
(909) 882-1344

National Association of State
    Coordinators for the Education of
    Homeless Children and Youth
1710 N. Congress Ave.
Austin, TX 78758
(512) 463-9067

National Center for Missing and
    Exploited Children
1835 K St., N.W. Suite 600
Washington, DC 20006
(703) 235-3900

National Child Abuse Hotline
(800) 4 A CHILD

National Coalition Against Domestic
    Violence
P.O. Box 34103
Washington, DC 20043-4103
(202) 638-6388

National Committee for the
    Prevention of Child Abuse
332 S. Michigan Ave., Suite 11600
Chicago, IL 60604
(312) 663-3520

National Crime Prevention Council
1700 K St., N.W., 2nd floor
Washington, DC 20006-3817
(202) 466-6272

National Safe Kids Campaign
111 Michigan Ave., N.W.
Washington, DC 20010
(202) 939-4993

National Student Campaign Against
    Hunger
29 Temple Place
Boston, MA 02111
(617) 292-4823

Neighborhood Watch (crime)
Contact your local police.
Pamplet available from:
American Security Education
P.O. Box 1337
Downey, CA 90240
(310) 928-1847

Parents Anonymous
520 S. Lafayette Park Place,
   Suite 316
Los Angeles, CA 90057
(213) 388-6685

Points of Light Foundation
1737 H St., N.W.
Washington, DC 20006
(800) 879-5400

Prison Fellowship
1856 Old Reston Ave.
Reston, VA 22090
(703) 478-0100

Kids Care Club Sample Forms

Kids Care Club Volunteer Registration

Name ———————————————— Date ————

Address ———————————————— Birthdate ————

———————— ———— ————
Town   State   Zip

Phone ——————————

School ——————————————————

What are your special interests?

For example: Do you like young children? Are you concerned about hunger? How do you feel about the homeless? Do you want to help the elderly? What suffering tugs at your heart strings?

————————————————————————————

————————————————————————————

————————————————————————————

————————————————————————————

What are your special skills?

Yes No
☐   ☐   Can you type?
☐   ☐   Do you like to paint walls/houses?
☐   ☐   Do you draw well?
☐   ☐   Can you do lawn/garden work?
☐   ☐   Do you know how to use the library?
☐   ☐   Can you cook?
☐   ☐   Can you wash windows?
☐   ☐   Can you write well?
☐   ☐   Are you a good people organizer?
☐   ☐   Can you teach younger kids?

Other: _____

_____

_____

When are you available to help? _____

— — — — — — — — — **Parent Section** — — — — — — —

Parents must acknowledge that Kids Care Club is a group of children helping their community and world. Parents must provide the supervision and support that their individual children need. The Kids Care Club is not responsible for the safety or supervision of any child. Please make informed decisions about the activities that your kids participate in, and the amount of support they need from you.

Parent Information:

	Mom	Dad
Parent names	_____	_____
Phone at work	_____	_____
Phone at home	_____	_____
Signature	_____	_____
Date	_____	_____

Any medical or other concerns which Club facilitators should know about:

_____

_____

Kids Care Club Project Worksheet

Project Planning

Whom will we help and on what date?

How long will the project take?

What preparations are necessary prior to the project date?

How many adults are needed?

What supplies are needed?

How many kids do we expect to participate?

Spreading the Word

- Hand out invitations via kids in school.
- Place a public service ad in your local paper.
- Hang posters around school and in local stores.
- Ask the principal to announce the project on the loud speaker.
- Write an article about the Club for the school newspaper.

Things to Remember on the Project Day

Sign-in Sheet:

> Make sure all the kids sign in. The names will be used for your newspaper article and for updating your membership list.

Name Tags:

> It's nice to feel connected with other human beings, and something as simple as a name tag can provide a personal connection.

Newspaper Photos:

> Take a couple of pictures when the project is finished with all the Kids Care Club members included. This group photo should be submitted to the local newspaper, along with a note that lists all of the kids' names (this is where the sign-in sheet is invaluable) and a brief description of what your project accomplished. Be sure you put your name and phone number on the back of the photo, in case the editor wants more information.

Kids Care Service Request Form

Date:

Dear Social Service Organization,

We would like to help you meet the needs of our community. We are the KIDS CARE CLUB. We are enthusiastic, energetic kids between the ages of five and eighteen. We work in teams of two or more, and have a variety of interests and ability levels. We are concerned about human suffering and want to make a difference in our community.

With a little training, we can do almost anything that adults can do, and we learn fast!

Your organization is invited to enter our network as a volunteer opportunity. Just fill out the Service Request Form below and mail it in. Also send any brochures or flyers that describe your organization and the needs you try to meet. We'll contact you when a volunteer team has been matched with your service request.

The KIDS CARE CLUB does not solicit grants or donations. We have no operating costs. Our goal is to strengthen the existing social service organizations in their war against human suffering.

KIDS CARE CLUB
Kids Can Make a Difference in the World

SERVICE REQUEST FORM   Date _____

Organization: _____

Address: _____

_____

Contact Person: _____ Phone:_____

How can we serve or assist your organization? Please be specific.

_____

_____

_____

_____

Send this form to the **KIDS CARE CLUB** at:

The Helping Skills Assessment Test

Put the number of skill points that apply to you on the line beside the task:

Skill Points

4	I can do it well	2	I can learn to do it
3	I can do it okay	1	I can't do it at all

Tasks

_____ Write a letter
_____ Paint a wall
_____ Sweep a floor
_____ Make phone calls
_____ Work with wood
_____ Read out loud
_____ Baby-sit
_____ Sand wooden blocks
_____ Make a sandwich
_____ Hand out flyers
_____ Be friendly—talk and listen
_____ Weed a garden
_____ Make bread
_____ Walk a nature trail
_____ Draw a picture
_____ Ask questions— interview
_____ Speak up against injustice
_____ Make cookies
_____ Take dictation
_____ Do art projects
_____ Paint toys
_____ Wash cribs
_____ Be friendly

_____ Clip coupons
_____ Speak another language
_____ Plan activities
_____ Use a tape recorder
_____ Pick up trash
_____ Sell things
_____ Shop for bargains
_____ Wash and set hair
_____ Iron clothing
_____ Do errands
_____ Type
_____ Use a computer
_____ Make coffee
_____ Heat a pot of soup
_____ Push a swing
_____ Rake a yard
_____ Teach a craft or skill
_____ Teach a game
_____ Sew
_____ Mow a lawn
_____ Answer a phone
_____ Sing songs
_____ Recruit new volunteers
_____ Teach ABC's to preschoolers

_____ Plant a garden
_____ Organize people
_____ Use a video camera
_____ Use puppets
_____ Ask for things
_____ Play a sport
_____ Use sign language
_____ Use the library
_____ Use a camera

_____ Address envelopes
_____ Work with young
children
_____ Work with the elderly
_____ Work with the
handicapped
_____ Dust a table
_____ Tighten a bolt
_____ Repair a torn book

Add up all your points. What are your total helping skill points? _____

If you have:

189–256 points = You have expert skills for helping others.

121–188 points = You are an advanced volunteer, with advanced skills.

64–120 points = Take the test again when you are in a better mood.

How Much Time Can You Spare?

Most kids have lots of activities to factor into their weekly schedule. What do you have to do each week? Do you have homework every day? Music lessons? Scout meetings? Church activities? Sports? Chores? A part-time job? What about time to hang around with friends? Go to parties? Go shopping? Sometimes our heart tells us one thing (example: "You should volunteer to help these people") while our brain tells us something else (example: "But I have three tests in school this week"). Be realistic when you volunteer to help others. Set your priorities. Perhaps some of the things on your schedule could be skipped if your volunteer work seems more important. But other things cannot be sacrificed, even for a good cause. Your volunteer job will be more fun and more fulfilling if you consider all your activities before you commit yourself to anything else. The following chart will help you determine when you have free time that could be used for volunteer work.

	8–10 A.M.	10 A.M.–12 P.M.	12–2 P.M.	2–4 P.M.	4–6 P.M.	6–8 P.M.
Monday						
Tuesday						
Wednesday						
Thursday						
Friday						
Saturday						
Sunday						

Fill in the time blocks that are used for school, homework, friends, sports, family or church. For example:

	8–10 A.M.	10 A.M.–12 P.M.	12–2 P.M.	2–4 P.M.	4–6 P.M.	6–8 P.M.
Monday	school	school	school	sports	homework	family
Tuesday	school	school	school		homework	family
Wednesday	school	school	school	sports	homework	family
Thursday	school	school	school		homework	family
Friday	school	school	school	sports	friends	friends
Saturday	sports				friends	friends
Sunday	church	church			homework	family

Kids Care Club Sign-in Sheet

Date: _____   **Project:** _____

Name	Address	Phone
1. _____	_____	_____
2. _____	_____	_____
3. _____	_____	_____
4. _____	_____	_____
5. _____	_____	_____
6. _____	_____	_____
7. _____	_____	_____
8. _____	_____	_____
9. _____	_____	_____
10. _____	_____	_____
11. _____	_____	_____
12. _____	_____	_____
13. _____	_____	_____
14. _____	_____	_____
15. _____	_____	_____
16. _____	_____	_____
17. _____	_____	_____
18. _____	_____	_____
19. _____	_____	_____
20. _____	_____	_____
21. _____	_____	_____
22. _____	_____	_____
23. _____	_____	_____

Kids Care Publicity Worksheet

Kids love to see their name in print. A little article in the local newspaper shows children that the community is behind them. But publicity serves other purposes too. People who read about the Club in the newspaper may call with a special need that the kids can meet. Other people may be inspired to do a kind deed for someone themselves. Publicity is a great way to spread the spirit of charity. Following are some hints for easy, effective publicity.

    1. Call the local newspaper and ask to speak to an editor. Tell the editor about your Club and ask the following questions:

      a. Are they able to print photos of the kids working at a project?

_____

      b. What type of prints do they accept (black and white or color, any specific size)?

_____

      c. What information would they like you to include in the article?

_____

      d. Are there any deadlines you should know about?

_____

    2. Make sure you take a camera and notepad to each project and meeting. Take lots of photos and choose the one that shows most of the kids at work. Use the notepad to record quotes from the kids or from the people they are helping. You can use the quotes in the article.

    3. Writing an article should not be intimidating. One paragraph is sufficient. It is important to include the names of the kids who participated in the event. (This is where the sign-

in sheet comes in handy.) Also, information on the project itself should be included, as well as information on the next project you have planned. Quotes from the kids at work, the people you are helping, and even passersby can provide interesting detail for the article. Following is a sample article from a Kids Care project.

NEW CANAAN, CONN., THURSDAY, JANUARY 23, 1992

More kids caring

The Kids Care Club is experiencing some growing pains. The Club originally met in the Spaides' kitchen on Weeburn Drive. But so many kids in New Canaan wanted to join the efforts to help the homeless and hungry, that the Club outgrew the kitchen ... and the living room and the dining room! Saxe Middle School offered the Kids Care Club use of the cafeteria on the third Saturday of every month and last Saturday the kids had their first meeting there. After making 150 bologna, cheese and lettuce sandwiches, they discussed ways they could help the homeless, elderly and needy children in the community. Attending were Lauren Brown, Casey Everett, Camila Pieratti, Erin West, Joan Davis, Rachel Schmidt, Christina DeMichele, Jennifer DeMichele, Julianne DeMichele, Patty Buckley, Jenny Spaide, Michelle Spaide, Heather Spaide, Gail Davidson, Liz Livingston, Melanie Heath, Michelle Heath and Katie Checkettes. Also changing is the Club's name for the high school students who participate. (It seems the high school participants would prefer a name without reference to kids.). There have been a few suggestions, but no final choice has been made.

Notes

1. Alan Luks and Peggy Payne, *The Healing Power of Doing Good* (New York, Fawcett, 1991).

2. Excerpt from *Magnificent Obsession* by Lloyd C. Douglas. Copyright 1929 by Houghton Mifflin Company and renewed 1957 by Betty Douglas Herman and Virginia Douglas Dawson. Reprinted by permission of Houghton Mifflin Company. All rights reserved.

3. Charles Murray, *Losing Ground* (New York, Basic Books, 1984), p. 189.

4. Center for Budget and Policy Priorities, Washington, D.C.

5. Conference of Mayor's Task Force on Hunger and Homelessness (Charleston, S.C.) 1989 survey.

6. National Alliance to End Homelessness, *What You Can Do to Help the Homeless* (New York, Simon & Schuster, 1991), p. 11.

7. Ibid., p. 42.

8. Marcia Brown, *Stone Soup* (New York, Scribner, 1947).

9. National Center for Health Statistics, Public Health Services, U.S. Dept. of Health and Human Services (Hyattsville, MD) 1991 figures.

10. Food, Research and Action Center, 1991, Washington, D.C.

11. National Alliance to End Homelessness, *What You Can Do to Help The Homeless* (New York, Simon & Schuster, 1991), p. 17.

12. Robert N. Butler, M.D., *Why Survive* (New York, Harper and Row, 1975), p. 25.

13. Dr. Paul Tournier, *Learning to Grow Old* (New York, Harper and Row, 1972).

14. National Center for Health Statistics, Public Health Services, U.S. Dept. of Health and Human Services (Hyattsville, MD) 1991 figures.

15. Sally L. Smith, *Succeeding Against the Odds* (Los Angeles, Tarcher, 1991), p. 2.

16. Betty B. Osman, *No One to Play With* (New York, Random House, 1982), p. 20.

Index

275